The Ultimate Vietnamese Cookbook

111 Dishes From Vietnam To Cook Right Now

Slavka Bodic

Imprint: Independently published

Please sign up for free Balkan and Mediterranean recipes:
www.balkanfood.org

Introduction

Vietnamese cuisine is rich in vegetables, herbs, and fruits, making it one of the healthiest cuisines on the planet. Savory spices blend refreshing flavors to create dishes with a nuanced taste, brilliant color, and appealing aroma. Vietnamese main meals are a staple of the cuisine and are typically served with rice or noodles. They can stand alone or as part of a multi meal, based on whether the dish is casual and at-home, festive, or communal.

Vietnamese mains are delightfully diverse in taste and texture, ranging from more well-known meals like Shaking Beef (B Lc Lc) to something more basic like Fried Tofu in Tomato Sauce (u St Cà Chua). Whether it's a soup, rice, or noodle dish, our main dish dishes will give the distinct, satiating, and nutrient-rich flavor you've come to expect from Vietnamese cuisine.

Vietnamese cuisine has received extensive coverage in international media. According to *The New York Times*, this is the "new culinary star of Asia" and one of the world's top ten cuisines. Thus, CNN has featured Vietnamese cuisine several times. Vietnam's restaurants and culinary festivals are drawing an increasing number of persons, and the number of international tourists visiting Vietnam to learn how to cook is growing.

Some even come to learn the language in order to create a Vietnamese restaurant. To me, the distinction between what constitutes an authentic Vietnamese meal as a major dish versus an appetizer or snack is hazy.

There are several foods that might be classified as a side dish or a snack, such as fresh spring rolls, egg rolls, banh cuon, or even banh mi.

What if you only have five spring rolls or add some egg rolls with dipping sauce to noodles, or quickly double your banh cuon recipe and add cha lua to it? In my opinion, you'll get an instant supper. In fact, I eat all of the Vietnamese major meals listed below as main courses, but I attest that several also work well as appetizers!

Yes, ordering Vietnamese takeout is the most convenient method to sample the country's traditional cuisine. However, if you really want the best experience, go handmade. That being said, here are 21 Vietnamese recipes that you may create at home. Buckle up and prepare to travel to Vietnam with your taste sensations!

TABLE OF CONTENTS

Vietnamese Cuisine

Vietnam cuisine is a special cultural synthesis of three distinct areas. Each region has its unique flavor and particular delicacies. This contributes to the variety and depth of Vietnamese culinary tradition. *The New York Times* food reviewer Marion Burros praised Vietnamese cuisine as "aromatic and spicy but subtle, with clean crisp flavors." Vietnamese people enjoy contrasting sweet and sour, hot and chilly, cooked and raw, and crispy and silky.

Southern Vietnamese cuisine are hotter, sweeter, oilier, with more exotic fruits and vegetables and MSGs than Northern Vietnamese foods, which are more influenced by French and Chinese cooking methods. Vietnamese food is notable for its use of fish sauce, soy sauce, rice, fresh fruits and vegetables, as well as herbs and spices such as lemon grass, lime, and kaffir lime leaves.

Fresh vegetables and herbs are always served as side dishes alongside dipping sauce in all regions of Vietnam. Pork, chicken, shrimp, cockles, and several other types of shellfish are the most commonly utilized meats in Vietnamese cuisine. Beef is commonly utilized in one of Vietnam's most famous foods, pho soup, as well as the 'seven course beef' feast.

Vietnamese food typically offers the following characteristics and features:

- Food freshness: Many meats are just briefly cooked. Vegetables are consumed raw; if cooked, they're boiled or briefly stir-fried.

- Herbs and vegetables: Herbs and vegetables are crucial in many Vietnamese meals and are frequently used in abundance.
- Broths and soup-based foods are popular.
- Vietnamese condiments are typically vibrant and organized in visually appealing patterns.

Sometimes pho is eaten for breakfast. Salty rice flour cakes with minced pork and dried shrimp are also famous. Breakfast may consist of porridge or French bread with jam and tea for the more Americanized Vietnamese. Lunch could include bahn mi, a sandwich of carrots, cilantro, onions, and daikon on a French roll with pork or chicken; rice vermicelli; or pork and veggies wrapped in thin rice-paper wrappers.

Dinner is nearly usually rice with a few steamed or stir-fried items, typically veggies and either fish or pig. The most frequent protein in the Vietnamese diet is fish. They cook fish in a range of methods, including steamed, sautéed, and fried. Pork and chicken are also popular in the United States, where meat is less expensive than in Vietnam.

Cabbage, gai lan (Chinese broccoli), mustard greens, collard greens, and cucumbers are common veggies. The most prevalent condiment is nuoc mam - fish sauce (made from salted and fermented anchovies), which is used in Vietnamese cookery in the same way that Americans use salt and Chinese use soy sauce. Most people use MSG in their cooking as well. France's influence can be clearly noticed in Vietnamese cuisine.

Most restaurants serve crème caramel; baguettes, croissants, and Vietnamese copies of French pastries are accessible in every market and downtown area, particularly in Hanoi and the north. Snails can even be found in some regions. French-Vietnamese cuisine is a culinary joy. The balance of all these parts is the secret of Vietnamese cuisine. Different amounts of components and spices produce various recipes and flavors.

Vietnam

Vietnam is a long, narrow Southeast Asian country. It's bordered to the North by China, to the west by Cambodia, Laos, and the Gulf of Thailand, and to the east by the South China Sea (which the Vietnamese call "the East Sea"). Vietnam is roughly the same size as Italy and Japan, with a total area of 327,500 square kilometers (126,500 square miles).

Vietnam's cuisine is heavily influenced by the country's topography. Rice is grown across the state, but mainly in the Red River delta in the North and the Mekong River delta in the South. In reality, the Vietnamese describe their country as a bamboo pole with a basket of rice at each end (the narrow core region).

Despite the fact that ¾ of Vietnam's territory is hilly or mountainous, the country's extensive seacoast and numerous inland canals produce fish and other aquatic creatures that are staples in the Vietnamese diet. Vietnamese cuisine varies slightly depending on area, with Chinese influences (such as stir fries, noodles, and the use of chopsticks) in the North and Cambodian (Khmer) and French influences in the South.

Climate influences the accessibility of products, which influences the types of cuisines that predominate in a certain region. During the winter months in the North, families congregate over a large bowl of seasoned broth to cook vegetables and meat in. A fish dish called cha ca, which is cooked in a comparable manner, is also popular. The charcoal brazier (small barbecue-style heat source) that keeps the broth boiling sits on the table and keeps everyone warm.

The traditional diet in the South, where the environment allows for a longer growing season and more foodstuffs are accessible, includes a wide variety of fruits and vegetables. Sugar and sugarcane are used more frequently in the south than in the north. Cha tom is a famous dish in the south (shrimp wrapped in sugarcane).

Because of Vietnam's tropical environment, meals in the south are cooked for a shorter period of time than those in the north. In the north, stir fries and slow-cooking stews are popular, whereas in the south, most meals are rapidly barbecued or eaten raw. Vietnam is one of the world's most densely populated countries, with a rapidly expanding population of 104 million people in 2022. More land is cleared for agriculture as the population grows.

According to 2001 figures, less than 20% of the area remained forested, and 40% was deemed unfit for crop cultivation. Farmers clearing land quickly burn plants to create place for crops. They then use the land to the point where it is no longer fertile or appropriate for crop production. This method of farming, known as shifting agriculture (or "slash and burn"), is most common in the north and other parts of the world.

Too much fishing has depleted the number of fish in the waters surrounding Vietnam, and the coastal marine environment is also threatened by oilfield development in the South. Neighbors have influenced the Vietnamese people in regards to what they eat and how they cook. People from Mongolia who invaded Vietnam from the North in the 10th century brought beef with them.

This is how beef became part of the Vietnamese diet. Common Vietnamese beef dishes are pho bo (Beef Noodle Soup) and bo bay mon (Beef Cooked Seven Ways). The Chinese who dominated Vietnam for 1,000 years taught the Vietnamese people cooking techniques such as stir frying and deep frying, as well as the use of chopsticks. In the South, neighboring Laos, Cambodia, and Thailand introduced such ingredients as flat, Cambodian style egg noodles, spices, chili, and coconut milk.

Breakfast

Banh Mi Sandwich with Eggs and Sausage

Preparation time: 35 minutes
Cook time: 35 minutes
Nutrition facts (per serving): 877 Cal (56g fat, 46g protein, 6g fiber)

In this Vietnamese spin on the egg sandwich, handmade sausage is used, and it's much simpler to create than you would expect. There's no need to bother with casings; just combine the ground pork with the spices, shape the mixture into patties, and cook on a skillet.

Ingredients (4 servings)

2 teaspoons minced scallion (white part only)
2 teaspoons minced ginger
1 ½ teaspoons brown sugar
1 ½ teaspoons red-pepper flakes
1 ½ teaspoons minced garlic
1 ½ teaspoons kosher salt
¾ teaspoon freshly ground black pepper
¾ teaspoon fresh thyme leaves
¾ teaspoon fish sauce
1 ¼ lbs. ground pork
2 tablespoons vegetable oil, divided
8 large eggs
1 baguette, cut into four segments, split on one side, toasted
Mayonnaise, for serving
Sambal or hot sauce, for serving

Kosher salt

Freshly ground black pepper

1 avocado, pitted and sliced

1 jalapeño, seeded and julienned, to taste

Cilantro and mint leaves, for serving

Preparation

Combine all the ingredients for the sausage, except for the ground pork, in a large bowl and stir until well combined. Mix in the meat until everything is well-combined. Make 8 patties from the pork mixture, each containing ⅓ cup of pork mixture. Add 1 tablespoon of oil to a medium-sized pan and heat it over medium-high heat. Cook the sausage patties in 2 batches, one at a time, until done and lightly browned, approximately 2 minutes each side.

The second batch should have 1 tablespoon oil added. Remove the sausage patties to a platter and drain the pan of all but 2 tablespoons of grease. Fry the eggs in batches in a medium-high pan until they are the desired doneness. Slice baguettes in half and put mayonnaise on the insides. If desired, spread the sambal on the top side of the bun. Top each sandwich with 2 sausage patties and 2 cooked eggs. Garnish and serve with avocado, jalapenos, cilantro, and mint.

Traditional Vietnamese Egg Coffee

Preparation time: 5 minutes
Cook time: 5 minutes
Nutrition facts (per serving): 175 Cal (5.5g fat, 7.8g protein, 0 g fiber)

A meringue-like, silky, smooth fluff may be produced by whipping one egg yolk into sweetened condensed milk. Add this to your coffee or iced coffee and you'll be sipping on a Vietnamese specialty.

Ingredients (1 servings)

1 large egg yolk
2 tablespoons sweetened condensed milk
½ cup hot strong coffee

Preparation

A large jar with egg yolk and condensed milk should be used to make this dish. Whip until soft peaks form using a milk frothier. Add frothed milk to a cup of steaming coffee.

Vietnamese Sandwich

Preparation time: 10 minutes

Cook time: 5 minutes

Nutrition facts (per serving): 627 Cal (12.1g fat, 55.3g protein, 3.3g fiber)

This is a dish that I learned from a local while working as an English teacher in Asia for many years. This banh mi sandwich from Vietnam is delicious and a welcome change from the usual fare. It's usual to find garlic chili sauce in Asian stores, but you may also use Indonesian sambal or Korean chili paste. This classic Vietnamese dish with French influences calls for beer or red wine as a beverage of choice.

Ingredients (4 servings)

4 boneless pork loin chops, cut ¼ inch thick

4 (7 inch) French bread baguettes, split lengthwise

4 teaspoons mayonnaise, or to taste

1-oz. chili sauce with garlic

¼ cup fresh lime juice

1 small red onion, sliced into rings

1 medium cucumber, peeled and sliced lengthwise

2 tablespoons chopped fresh cilantro

Salt and pepper, to taste

Preparation

The broiler should be preheated in the oven. Take out a broiler pan and place the pork chops on the pan. For a browned outside, cook for 5 minutes, flipping once. Spread mayonnaise on the insides of the French rolls. Put a cooked pork chop in each bun. Apply chili sauce to the meat immediately. Slices of onion, cucumber, cilantro, salt, and pepper are sprinkled on top. Add a last spritz of lime juice to complete the look.

Vietnamese Crepes (Banh Xeo)

Preparation time: 20 minutes
Cook time: 5 minutes
Nutrition facts (per serving): 788 Cal (45.2g fat, 21.5g protein, 20.1g fiber)

Vietnam's southern provinces are known for their love of bahn xeo (pronounced bahn SAY-oh). Swirling pancakes or crepes are what the term alludes to, and the sound they create when they strike a hot griddle inspired the name. Once the shrimp-filled crepe is wrapped in lettuce and dipped in nuoc cham, it's ready to be eaten. A garnish of fresh herbs is a nice touch.

Ingredients (5 servings)
1 cup rice flour
½ teaspoon white sugar
½ teaspoon salt
¼ teaspoon ground turmeric
1 cup coconut milk
½ cup water

Filling
2 tablespoons vegetable oil, divided, or as needed
2 tablespoons minced shallot
2 cloves garlic, minced, or more to taste
¾ lb. fresh shrimp, peeled and deveined
2 tablespoons fish sauce, or more to taste
Salt, to taste

1 lb. mung bean sprouts

4 lettuce leaves, or as needed

Preparation

In a large basin, combine rice flour, sugar, salt, and turmeric for the batter. Beat in the coconut milk until it forms a thick paste. A thin crepe batter is the ideal consistency for this recipe. Prepare the filling: In a large skillet, heat 1 ½ tablespoons of oil over medium-high heat. Add shallots and garlic; cook and stir until fragrant but not browned, about 1 to 2 minutes, then remove from the heat and set aside.

Sauté the shrimp for 3 to 4 minutes, or until they are opaque and cooked through. Salt and fish sauce should be added to the mix. Add the filling to a bowl and mix it all together. The oven should be preheated at 200 degrees Fahrenheit (95 degrees C). Reheat over medium heat after cleaning the skillet. Pour in the remaining 1 ½ teaspoons of oil and mix well. Pour half a cup of crepe batter onto a heated pan, stirring to coat the bottom, and cook until golden brown. On the bottom half of the crepe, place 3 or 4 cooked shrimp.

Add a few bean sprouts on top for color and crunch. Batter will be ready when it seems set and begins to brown around the edges, which will take around 1 minute to achieve. Slide crepe onto an oven-safe dish and flip it over. To keep the crepe warm, place it in the oven. Cook the remaining crepes in the same manner. Serve a serving of lettuce with the crepes that have been filled. In order to consume, tear off a piece of crepe and wrap it up in some lettuce.

Vietnamese Shrimp Pancakes (Banh Xeo)

Preparation time: 20 minutes
Cook time: 30 minutes
Nutrition facts (per serving): 416 Cal (58.8g fat, 22.7g protein, 2.8g fiber)

Even if you live somewhere that doesn't have a wonderful Vietnamese restaurant, you can still enjoy these flavorful pancakes. You can't go wrong with an omelet stuffed with shrimp and pig chops. If you're serving them in the cooler months, they'll be perfect for warming up a cold autumn or winter evening.

Ingredients (4 servings)
20 medium (blank)s uncooked medium shrimp, peeled and deveined
5 oz. boneless pork loin, sliced
1 teaspoon fish sauce
1 pinch monosodium glutamate (MSG)
⅔ cup rice flour
7 oz. water
6 oz. coconut milk
3 medium (4-⅛" long) s green onions, finely chopped
½ teaspoon saffron
2 cups vegetable oil for frying, or as needed
½ cup bean sprouts
2 tablespoons chopped fresh basil

Chili Sauce

½ cup lime juice

⅓ cup fish sauce

3 tablespoons water

3 tablespoons white sugar

2 dried red chili peppers, chopped

2 cloves garlic, crushed

1 pinch monosodium glutamate (MSG)

4 leaves mustard greens

Preparation

For 30 minutes, marinate the shrimp and pork loin in a glass or ceramic dish with the fish sauce and MSG. Mix rice flour, water, coconut milk, green onions, and saffron powder. In a medium-sized saucepan, heat 1 tablespoon of vegetable oil over medium heat. When bubbles begin to form, flip and cook for another 3 to 4 minutes until the edges are dry.

On the pancake, spread a quarter of the shrimp and pork mixture. Reduce heat to medium, add ¼ of the bean sprouts and basil, turn, and cook until browned on the other side, 2 to 3 minutes. To serve, fold the pancake in half and place on a serving dish. Repeat this process with the remaining batter and filling. Mix lime juice, fish sauce, water, sugar, red chili peppers, garlic, and MSG for sauce together. In order to consume, wrap the pancakes together in a mustard green leaf and dip in the sauce.

Breakfast Crepes

Preparation time: 20 minutes
Cook time: 10 minutes
Nutrition facts (per serving): 216 Cal (3.1g fat, 9.1g protein, 1g fiber)

This breakfast is excellent and easy to make in the morning. Butter, sugar, jam, or chocolate spread are all acceptable accompaniments. Enjoy!

Ingredients (servings)
1 cup all-purpose flour
1 cup milk
1 egg
1 pinch salt

Preparation
Mix the flour, milk, egg, and salt into a medium-sized bowl. Ensure a big frying pan or wok has been heated to a high temperature in the stovetop. In order to get the pan hot enough, add a teaspoon of butter and gently coat it in the melted butter.

Using a circular motion, pour one-fourth of a cup of batter into the pan and tilt it to evenly distribute the batter. The crepe should be browning after 2 minutes, so pick up one edge with a spatula to check. Flip the crepe when the bottom has started to brown and cook the second side for approximately 2 minutes or until it has also browned. To cook the remaining crepes, use the same methods as before. Serve warm.

Vietnamese Prawn Omelets

Preparation time: 20 minutes
Cook time: 30 minutes
Nutrition facts (per serving): 523 Cal (19g fat, 25g protein, 2g fiber)

This prawn omelets delivers a flavorful punch thanks to a zesty Vietnamese sauce drizzled on top.

Ingredients (4 servings)
8 eggs
3 teaspoon fish sauce
3 oz. butter
⅓ cup peanut oil
24 green king prawns, peeled, cleaned
1 red onion, finely chopped
1 large carrot, cut into julienne (matchsticks)
2 spring onions, thinly sliced on the diagonal
2 long red chili peppers, seeded, cut into julienne
1 cup loosely packed coriander leaves

Dressing
2 limes, juiced
2 cloves garlic, crushed
1 tablespoon fish sauce
1 tablespoon caster sugar
1 long red chili pepper, seeded, finely chopped

Preparation

You'll need a small bowl and some whisking to prepare the dressing. Whisk eggs, fish sauce, and 2 tablespoons of cold water together in a bowl to form omelets. Cook the onion and garlic in 1 tablespoon oil and ⅓ oz. of butter on a medium-high heat frying pan. Cook, stirring occasionally, for 2 ½ minutes or until the prawns are pink, 6 prawns and a quarter of the onion. Add ¼ of the egg mixture using a ladle. Add salt and pepper to taste.

During the last 5 minutes of cooking, make sure the omelet is set and the prawns are just cooked through. To keep the omelet warm, place it on a dish and tent it loosely with aluminum foil. To finish, add the remaining egg mixture and prawns to the pan. Salad ingredients: mix half the dressing with the carrots and spring onions and coriander; toss thoroughly. Top the omelets with the salad mixture and serve. To serve, drizzle with the remainder of the dressing.

Soups and Stews

Crabmeat and Asparagus Soup

Preparation time: 10 minutes
Cook time: 45 minutes
Nutrition facts (per serving): 100 Cal (3 g fat, 16.2 g protein, 0.9 g fiber)

It's a beautiful mix of tastes that complement one another. Surprisingly. I saw a similar recipe on the internet (not here) and modified it by removing the unusual ingredients (which I'm unable to identify or get). It's Vietnamese in origin. You can tell it's good for you since it's light and refreshing.

Ingredients (4 servings)
4 cups chicken stock or prepared broth
1 teaspoon peeled and minced fresh ginger
½ lb. asparagus spears, trimmed and cut on the diagonal into 1-inch pieces
1 egg, well beaten
1 tablespoon cornstarch mixed with 2 tablespoon water
2 teaspoon dry sherry
1 teaspoon Asian sesame oil
1 teaspoon soy sauce
1 cup cooked crabmeat, picked over for shell fragments

Preparation
Bring the stock and ginger to a roaring boil in a large pot over high heat. Cook for around 3 minutes until the asparagus is done but still crisp-tender before removing the lid and serving. Reduce the temperature to a

simmer. Beat the egg and add 2 tablespoons of the heated stock to it. Pour the egg mixture into the stock in a slow, steady stream while continually swirling to ensure that the cooked egg threads are equal. Add the sherry, sesame oil, and soy sauce to the cornstarch mixture. Cook for approximately a minute, stirring constantly, until the soup has thickened somewhat. Add the crabmeat and simmer for 2 to 3 minutes, until it's warmed through. Adjust the spices to your liking after tasting. Serve the soup hot, straight from the pot.

Pork Rib Soup with Kabocha

Preparation time: 30 minutes

Cook time: 25 minutes

Nutrition facts (per serving): 411 Cal (5.5 g fat, 25.7 g protein, 0.6 g fiber)

Soup prepared with creamy kabocha squash, turkey meatballs, shiitake mushrooms, shrimp and chicken broth make a satisfying meal. Fresh scallions and cilantro are sprinkled on top of the soup. Serve with jasmine rice, fish sauce, and chopped Thai chili peppers in a small dish on the side.

Ingredients (5 servings)

2-3 tablespoons vegetable oil

1 teaspoon minced garlic

1 lb. pork bones or spare ribs cut into bite-size pieces (blanch in boiling water with 1 teaspoon salt for 5 minutes, then rinse)

4 cups water

1 ½ lbs. kabocha squash flesh cut into bite-size pieces (with or without skin)

2 ½ teaspoon salt

4 teaspoons white granulated sugar

3 teaspoons chicken/mushroom/pork stock powder

Pinch black pepper

2-3 green onions (remove stems, cut into 1-inch segments)

Preparation

Add some vegetable oil to the bottom of the small pot. The temperature should be set to medium-low. Add some garlic. Stir until the aroma is intoxicating (about 15 seconds). Add pig bones or ribs. In a large bowl, combine pork bones, garlic, and seasoning. Add water to the mixture. Once it's boiling, turn the heat down. 30 minutes of simmering is the recommended time. Remove the foam from the top if necessary. Include the kabocha. Squash should be tender enough to penetrate easily with a knife, but not so soft that it falls apart, about 5-10 minutes. Black pepper and stock powder are excellent additions to any dish. Remove the pan from the heat and garnish with chopped green onions. Serve with steamed rice for a full dinner or as a side dish for a snack.

Vegetable Soup with Pig Skin

Preparation time: 40 minutes

Cook time: 15 minutes

Nutrition facts (per serving): 138 Cal (2.6g fat, 9.5 g protein, 3.2 g fiber)

Vietnam has a long-standing culinary heritage that includes vegetable soup with pig skin. This meal is often prepared for special occasions, such as feast days or the Tet festival. The delicate nature of traditional Vietnamese cuisine is reflected in its vivid colors, crisp flavor, and sophisticated method of preparation, all of which are present in this dish.

Ingredients (4 servings)

Broth

1 lb. chicken bones

3 cloves red shallots

1 knob ginger

2 scallions

Soup

2 oz. carrots

2 oz. kohlrabi

3 ½ oz. broccoli

2 oz. snow peas

2 oz. mushrooms

3 ½ oz. dried pig skin

10 quail eggs

Coriander pepper, salt, fish sauce and sugar, to taste

Preparation

Cut the kohlrabi and the carrot into small pieces. Allow the dry pig skin sheet to soften in warm water. Ginger juice may be made by chopping the ginger and mixing it with wine. The pigskin should be squeezed into the mixture before it is added. Once again, scrub the pig skin with a mild detergent. Set aside bite-sized chunks of the meat for later use. Peel the quail eggs and put them aside. Bring the chicken bone broth to a boil in a saucepan. Immediately take the saucepan contents and set them in the dish with the quail eggs. Cook for approximately 30 seconds, then remove the saucepan contents and place them with the quail eggs in a separate bowl. Pour the soup into the bowl after marinating it with fish sauce, salt, and a little sugar.

Spicy Vietnamese Beef and Noodle Soup

Preparation time: 20 minutes
Cook time: 5 hours 15 minutes
Nutrition facts (per serving): 390 Cal (14.5g fat, 30g protein, 1.4g fiber)

Here's a substantial soup similar to stew that is modeled by the Vietnamese pho. The spicy and sour components are delicious when combined with Asian beer. Begin making this soup 24 hours before you want to serve it. My attempt at the traditional Vietnamese beef noodle soup known as Pho is included inside this recipe. To finish, garnish with raw beef tenderloin that has been cut very thinly, basil, mint, cilantro, chile sambal, and fresh wedges of lime.

Ingredients (8 servings)
1 tablespoon vegetable oil
2 thick slices beef shank
2 lbs. beef oxtail, cut into pieces
1 (6 inch) piece fresh ginger, sliced
6 whole star anise
1 teaspoon fennel seed
1 teaspoon whole coriander seeds
2 whole cloves
1 cinnamon stick
1 cardamom pod
3 quarts water
1 onion, halved
6 cloves garlic

2 tablespoons white sugar

1 bay leaf

2 tablespoons fish sauce

1 tablespoon soy sauce

1 (16 oz.) package fresh rice noodles

1 cup fresh bean sprouts, or to taste

1 fresh jalapeno pepper, sliced into rings, or to taste

Preparation

To preheat the oil, place it in a big saucepan and set it over medium-high heat. Cook the beef shank, oxtail pieces, and ginger in the heated oil, turning them regularly until they are browned, which should take between three and five minutes each side. Sauté the anise star, fennel seed, coriander seed, cloves, cinnamon stick, and cardamom pod in the saucepan until the aroma of the spices is released, which should take around 30 seconds. Mix the water, onion, garlic, white sugar, and bay leaf into the beef mixture. Bring to a boil, then decrease the heat to a low setting and simmer for 5 to 6 hours, or until the broth is delicious and the meat is coming from the bone. Remove the meat, and set it aside.

Pour the strained veggies and seasonings back into the saucepan, but save the broth itself. The beef shank flesh should be chopped and added to the saucepan with the broth. Next, fish sauce and soy sauce should be stirred in. Bring the broth up to a simmer, then turn the heat down to a low setting to keep it warm. Rice noodles should be placed in a big bowl and then covered with boiling water. Set aside for approximately 5 minutes, or until the noodles have softened. After draining, rinsing with cold water is recommended. Put a handful of bean sprouts in the bottom of a big dish that can hold soup. Place a huge handful of cooked rice noodles on top of the dish, and then scatter a few slices of jalapeño over the noodles. Pour enough beef stock into the dish to cover the noodles completely.

Vietnamese Style Shrimp Soup

Preparation time: 15 minutes
Cook time: 20 minutes
Nutrition facts (per serving): 212 Cal (4.7 g fat,14.4 g protein, 2.7g fiber)

This one is quite easy to make and has the flavor of a traditional Vietnamese soup. Before adding anything to the pot, make sure that all of your components have been prepared; the cooking time for this soup is really short.

Ingredients (6 servings)

1 tablespoon vegetable oil

2 teaspoons minced fresh garlic

2 teaspoons minced fresh ginger root

1 (10 oz.) package frozen chopped spinach, thawed and drained

Salt and black pepper, to taste

2 quarts chicken stock

1 cup shrimp stock

1 teaspoon hot pepper sauce

1 teaspoon hoisin sauce

20 peeled and deveined medium shrimp

1 (6.75 oz.) package long rice noodles (rice vermicelli)

2 green onions, chopped

Preparation

In a big saucepan, heat the vegetable oil to medium-high heat. Stir in the garlic and ginger; simmer and stir for a further one-minute. Salt and pepper the spinach before serving. Cook the spinach, covered, for 3 minutes or until it's heated. Toss in the hot pepper sauce and hoisin sauce before adding the chicken and shrimp stock to the pot. Over medium heat, bring the mixture back to a simmer. Then add the shrimp and noodles when the soup is at a simmer. Stir in the green onions and continue cooking for another 5 minutes. Add salt and pepper to taste before serving.

Amandas Quick Pho

Preparation time: 10 minutes
Cook time: 10 minutes
Nutrition facts (per serving): 283 Cal (3.4 g fat, 20.4 g protein, 2 g fiber)

Adapted from a Vietnamese pho recipe, this one offers a few changes. Making this dish at home is a viable alternative to ordering takeout. Fresh basil, cilantro, bean sprouts, more hoisin sauce, and sriracha spicy sauce may be added to the dish for enriched flavor.

Ingredients (8 servings)
10 oz rice noodle, dried, narrow, and flat
Warm water, for soaking
1 tablespoon whole black peppercorn
1 tablespoon coriander seed
4 pods whole star anise
1-piece fresh ginger, 2-inch (5 cm) piece
1 bunch green onion
4 cups hot water
8 cups chicken broth
1 lb. chicken breast, halved, crosswise
¼ cup fish sauce
2 limes
1 jalapeño
1 bean sprout
1 bunch fresh Thai basil
1 bunch fresh cilantro

1 siracha

Hoisin sauce, to taste

Preparation

In a large heatproof bowl, combine the rice noodles and water. Soak for 20 minutes in warm water to soften. The big pot should be preheated to medium-high heat while the noodles are being soaked. For 2 minutes, heat the black peppercorns, coriander seeds, and star anise pods until aromatic. Peel and chop the ginger while the seeds are roasting. Trim the ends of the green onions, then cut the base of the onion by about 5 inches and keep the rest of the green tops for another use. Remove from heat after 2 minutes and let it cool slightly before chopping finely. Toss in the chicken breasts, water, and chicken broth, to taste. Cover and bring to a simmer over high heat.

Cook for a further 5 minutes, then keep an eye on it minute by minute until it's done. Don't let it get much hotter. Thinly slice the green onion tops while the soup is heating. Slice the lime in half. Slice the jalapeno into thin strips. Drain the rice noodles and add them back to the bowl after soaking for 20 minutes. Make sure the chicken is out of the soup. Discard the noodles and pour the soup over them. Mix in the fish sauce after re-inserting all of the noodles and stock back into the kettle. For 3 minutes, cover and cook. Cook the chicken until it is easily shred able. Top the noodles with the shredded chicken, jalapeno, bean sprouts, and Thai basil, and serve. Pour the hot pho soup over the noodles and serve immediately. Any additional preferred garnishes may be used, such as lime juice, green onions, and so on. Enjoy!

Instant Pot Beef Pho

Preparation time: 53 minutes

Cook time: 20 minutes

Nutrition facts (per serving): 367 Cal (8.7 g fat, 17.5 g protein, 0.8 g fiber)

The stock is the key to pho, the aromatic Vietnamese noodle soup with meat and tasty garnishes. Pressure cooking is the best way to create a good stock. This flavorful soup is made with fish sauce and toasted spices and prepared in just a few minutes using a pressure cooker. With an Instant Pot, you can boil the bones, sauté the aromatics, and finish the meal all in one pot. To serve, place small bowls of onion, bean sprouts, limes, and Thai basil on the table. Your guests may top their bowls of pho to their hearts' content.

Ingredients (6 servings)

3-star anise pods

3-inch cinnamon stick

4 whole cloves

2 tablespoons vegetable oil, plus more for noodles

2 medium onions, peeled, halved

2 inch piece ginger, scrubbed, sliced lengthwise ¼ inch thick

3 lb. mixed soup beef bones (oxtail, marrow, knuckles, and/or neck bone), rinsed under cold running water to remove blood and excess bits

1 lb. beef brisket or chuck, cut into 2-inch pieces

2 tablespoons (or more) fish sauce

½ oz. yellow rock sugar or 3 teaspoons granulated sugar

1 ¼ teaspoon kosher salt

10 oz. dried thin Banh Pho rice or similar noodles

8 oz. beef eye of round, sirloin steak, London broil, or tri-tip steak

Preparation

Sauté on high in a 6-quart Instant Pot. 2 minutes of swirling the spices will bring out the aroma and crackle of the star anise and cinnamon sticks. Work in 2 tablespoons of oil to coat the bottom of the saucepan. Reduce the heat to medium and sauté the onions and ginger, cut sides down, for 5–7 minutes, until deeply browned. Then, using a wooden spoon to scrape off any brown pieces, add 1 cup of water, followed by the bones and brisket as well as the fish sauce and sugar. Close the lid and tighten the venting knob. Pressure cooks for 1 hour at high pressure (it'll take about 20 minutes to come to pressure before the cook time begins). Relax for 30 minutes and let go of any tension. Cover noodles with cold water while the soup cooks. 30-minute soak. Remove extra starch from noodles. 20–30 minutes to freeze beef eye of round.

Slice thinly against the grain, then refrigerate. After 30 minutes, drape a cloth over the vent to avoid splattering. Open vent using a wooden spoon. When pin drops, open lid cautiously. Tong bones into a dish. Pour cold water over brisket to chill and prevent drying. Using a fine-mesh strainer, remove solids from broth; discard aromatics and reserve meat and bones. (Reserve leftover meat and bones for fried rice or bibimbap, or scoop out marrow and spread it over grilled toast.) Ladle fat off surface and discard. If required, add fish sauce or salt to stock. Low-simmer when cooking noodles. Bring a big pot of water to a rolling boil by filling it up about a third of the way. Chopsticks or a wooden spoon may be used to stir the noodles until they are just al dente, approximately 15 seconds. Rinse the noodles in a strainer with cold water to halt the cooking process.

Toss with a little oil after drizzling it on top Brisket should be drained and sliced thinly against the grain after it has been removed from the water. Serve the noodles in large dishes. Noodles may be added to bowls that have been warmed by swirling hot water around them. Stack the brisket, eye of round, and any remaining meat and bones (if using) on top of the sliced onion, scallions, and cilantro (if using) in each dish; season with pepper. Cook the meat by sprinkling hot broth on top of it. Set out on a tray with some garnish such as Thai basil leaves and mint leaves as well as mung bean sprouts, chili peppers, and lime slices for dipping.

Vietnamese Beef Pho

Preparation time: 10 minutes
Cook time: 1 hour 20 minutes
Nutrition facts (per serving): 528 Cal (13.6 g fat, 27.1g protein, 2g fiber)

This soup is served on a dish with fresh garnishes and different sauces. Fill a big saucepan with water. This gives each guest the opportunity to customize their meal to their liking. Because the meat is cooked in the bowl, the soup is a little out of the ordinary. The beef is cut so thinly that it's practically visible through the meat. The butcher may be able to slice it for you. The noodles and uncooked beef are drenched in the scalding soup. It just takes a few minutes for the meat to simmer in the boiling broth before it is garnished.

Ingredients (8 servings)

10 lb. mixed beef leg bones , shin, knuckle and marrow bones
12 oz ginger, 2 large hands, halved lengthwise
1 head large garlic, halved crosswise
8 lbs. medium yellow onion, halved lengthwise
8 sticks cinnamon
¼ cup whole black peppercorn
6 pods whole star anise
1 lb. beef brisket
Kosher salt, to taste
¼ cup fish sauce, plus more to taste
1 lb. boneless sirloin steak
1 lb. flat rice noodle, cooked according to package instructions

Servings

2 cups fresh mung bean sprouts

1 small red onion, very thinly sliced lengthwise

1 jalapeño, sliced into thin rounds

1 large bunch fresh Thai basil

1 lime, cut into wedges

Hoisin sauce

Siracha

Preparation

In a large stockpot, place the beef bones and cover with cold water by 2 inches (5 cm). For 10 minutes, bring the mixture to a boil over high heat and cook the bones to eliminate any impurities, blanching the bones. Preheat the broiler and place a rack in its uppermost position in the oven. Rinse the bones under cold running water in a colander. Add the blanched bones back into the stockpot and stir. Set up a rimmed baking sheet with the cut side up of the ginger, garlic, and onion and broil on high for 5 minutes.

Cooked vegetables should be added to the stockpot with the bones after they have been removed from the oven. Toss all of the spices together in a medium skillet over medium-high heat and toast for approximately 5 minutes, stirring regularly, until they begin to brown in patches and become quite aromatic. Pour in the roasted spices and bring to a simmer. Add the brisket to the stockpot and season it thoroughly with salt. Water should be added to the pot until everything is submerged by 1 inch (2 cm). As soon as the brisket is fork-tender, remove any excess fat from the surface by skimming off and discarding it as required. Cook for another 2-3 hours. Transfer the brisket to a platter and allow it to cool fully before cutting into it. Keep the brisket in the fridge until you're ready to eat it. 3-4 additional hours of simmering the soup to extract as much flavor as possible.

Remove the bones and aromatics with tongs and discard them. Slowly drain the broth in a big saucepan using a fine mesh strainer. The fish sauce should be added after the fat has been skimmed off the soup and discarded. If you like it, you can always add more. Slice the brisket very thinly. Slice the sirloin steak against the grain very thinly. Top the noodles with the brisket and raw steak before serving. Hot broth is ladled over noodles and beef and served with bean sprouts, onion jalapeno Thai basil lime wedges, hoisin sauce, and Sriracha as a side dish. Serve immediately. Enjoy!

Minhais Bitter Melon Soup

Preparation time: 15 minutes

Cook time: 30 minutes

Nutrition facts (per serving): 171 Cal (10.9g fat, 14.8g protein, 0.2g fiber)

Try this dish for pork and bitter melon made in the Vietnamese tradition that my buddy Minh-ai N. showed me how to prepare. Here's a traditional recipe that's enjoyed in both the Chinese and Vietnamese culinary traditions. Its unusually bitter taste is comparable to that of strong tea that hasn't been sweetened. You may serve the soup right away, or you can refrigerate it for up to a day. The taste of the soup will become less bitter after it has been refrigerated for a day. Serve hot, spooned over bowls of white rice that has been cooked.

Ingredients (3 servings)

½ lb. ground pork

2 tablespoons soy sauce

⅛ teaspoon garlic powder

⅛ teaspoon ground black pepper

1 bitter melon

4 cups water

1 teaspoon soy sauce, or to taste

1 teaspoon fish sauce, or to taste

1 green onions, sliced

Preparation

In a bowl, combine the ground pork with the garlic powder, pepper, and 2 tablespoons of soy sauce. Place the bowl, which has been covered with plastic wrap, in the refrigerator for anything between half an hour and a whole hour. Cut the bitter melon into rounds with a thickness of about 1 ½ inches. Take the point of a tiny knife and scrape off the seeded inside to reveal the spongy center. Make sure that each ring of bitter melon is thoroughly packed before proceeding with the next step. Fill each ring with the pork mixture. Make meatballs of about the same size out of any leftover pork. Put the water in a pot, and bring it up to a boil. Put in the packed rings of bitter melon, as well as any remaining meatballs. Simmer the bitter melon over a medium heat for 30 to 45 minutes, or until it can be easily sliced with a spoon and has reached a soft state. Take the pan off the heat. Add a pinch each of fish sauce and soy sauce to the seasoning mix. Stir in some green onions.

Chicken Pho

Preparation time: 10 minutes
Cook time: 30 minutes
Nutrition facts (per serving): 521 Cal (13.7g fat, 49.8g protein,13.7 g fiber)

This is definitely one of my top picks for soups. Going out to Vietnamese restaurants is one of my favorite things to do, but ever since I came up with this soup, we never leave the house!

Ingredients (2 servings)
¾ inch section ginger
2 medium-large green onions
1 very small bunch cilantro sprigs
1 ½ teaspoons coriander seeds
1 whole clove
4 cups low-sodium chicken broth
2 cups water
7 oz. boneless, skinless chicken breast or thighs
½ teaspoon fine sea salt
5 oz. dried narrow flat rice noodles
3 teaspoons fish sauce
½ teaspoon organic sugar or 1 teaspoon maple syrup (optional)
Pepper (optional)
Bean sprouts, mint sprigs, Thai basil, cilantro leaves, lime wedges, thinly-sliced chili peppers, to taste

Preparation

After peeling and slicing the ginger in a transverse direction, create 4 or 5 coins. Pound with the flat side of a knife. Set aside. Remove and put aside 2-3 tablespoons of the hollow green sections of the green onion. These should be cut into thin rounds. The remaining white portions should be cut into lengths about the size of a pinkie finger, then bruised and added to the ginger. Get 2 teaspoons of chopped cilantro leaves, coarsely cut the green tips of the cilantro, and put them aside. Keep the leftover cilantro sprigs aside for later use. Toast the clove and coriander seeds in a saucepan of 3 or 4 quarts set over medium heat for 1 to 2 minutes, or until the aroma is released. Add the combination of ginger and green onion, and stir for 30 seconds, or until the scent is released. After taking the pot off the heat and allowing it to cool for approximately a minute and a half, pour the stock in.

Bring the saucepan back up to temperature, then add the chicken, 2 cups of water, and the cilantro sprigs. Bring the liquid up to a boil over high heat. Turn the heat down to low and let the mixture simmer for half an hour. While the broth is heating up, prepare the rice noodles by soaking them in hot water until malleable and opaque. Drain, rinse, and put aside.

After 5 to 10 minutes of simmering, the chicken should be cooked all the way through and have a firm texture (it should yield slightly when pressed). Upon transferring the chicken to a dish, halt the cooking process by rinsing the bowl with cold water and then draining the chicken. Once it has cooled, chop or shred it into bits that are easily swallowed. To prevent the skin from drying out, cover it loosely. When the broth is finished, pour it through a strainer with a fine mesh and into a saucepan with a capacity of 2 quarts (line the strainer with muslin for a super-clear broth). Throw away all of the solids. You need to have around 4 cups of broth.

If desired, add a robust savory-sweet tone by using some fish sauce along with sugar or maple syrup. Bring the broth that has been strained to a boil over high heat. After placing the noodles in a noodle strainer or a mesh screen, immerse them for 5 to 60 seconds in the boiling broth so that they may heat up and soften. Take the noodles out of the saucepan and place them in 2 separate very big bowls. While arranging the chicken on top of the noodles and garnishing it with chopped green onion, chopped cilantro, and a sprinkle of pepper, reduce the heat to maintain the broth at a warm temperature. Before pouring the stock into the bowls, bring the broth back up to a boil. If you like, you may enjoy it with some basil, mint, sprouts, chili, and lime.

Chicken and Pineapple Soup

Preparation time: 1 hour
Cook time: 1 hour
Nutrition facts (per serving): 251 Cal (11g fat, 11g protein, 5g fiber)

The following was submitted by Kia Ly Dickinson of Miami, Florida: "This flavorful soup will send you into a tizzy because it is so delicious. With either hot or cold rice, it may be served either way. This dish is a tribute to my birthplace, Vietnam, and I'd want to share the recipe with some of my new friends in the United States." This recipe asks for fresh lemon verbena; however, in the event that fresh lemon verbena isn't available, you may use one stalk of fresh lemongrass in its place.

Ingredients (7 servings)

2 pineapples
8 cup water
2 tablespoons sunflower oil
2 tablespoons dried chili flakes red
3 teaspoon garlic cloves, minced
2 tablespoon fish sauce
1 lemongrass
4 oz. shiitake mushrooms, thinly sliced
2 tomatoes large, chopped
1 teaspoon freshly ground black pepper
2 chicken breast fillets
7 oz. noodles rice, softened
¼ cup fresh basil, roughly chopped
¼ cup fresh mint, chopped

Preparation

Pineapples should be peeled and cored before being thrown away, leaving just the skin. The cores should be chopped and then pureed in a blender with half a cup of water. To get the most liquid out of the mixture, strain it through a sieve while pushing down on the particles. Throw away the sediments, but save the fluid for later use. You should also chop the leftover chunks of pineapple and keep them aside. In a big saucepan, heat 1 tablespoon of oil, then sauté the chili flakes and 2 teaspoons of garlic for a minute or 2, until the mixture becomes aromatic. After another 2 minutes of cooking, stir in a quarter of a cup of fish sauce. First, add enough water to the pineapple juice so that you have a total of 8 cups, and then add the lemongrass stalk to the saucepan. Bring to a boil, then add the pineapple pieces that have been retained, mushrooms, tomatoes, and half a teaspoon of pepper. Bring the mixture back up to a boil, then reduce the heat, cover, and let it simmer for 10 minutes.

In the meanwhile, bring the remaining oil to a simmer in a frying pan. Add the remainder of the garlic, a sprinkle of red pepper flakes, and the 2 tablespoons of fish sauce that are still in the bottle. Cook for 2 minutes, or until the liquid has been reduced, before adding the chicken to the pan, seasoning it with a half teaspoon of pepper, and quickly frying it until cooked through. Cook the chicken in the broth for one minute after stirring it in. After dividing the noodles among the serving bowls, spoon the piping hot soup on top of each portion. Next, serve with the herbs having been chopped. Pineapples should be peeled and cored before being thrown away, leaving just the skin. The cores should be chopped and then pureed in a blender with ½ a cup of water. To get the most liquid out of the mixture, strain it through a sieve while pushing down on the particles. Throw away the sediments, but save the fluid for later use. You should also chop the leftover chunks of pineapple and keep them aside. In a big saucepan, heat 1 tablespoon of oil, then sauté the chilies and 2 teaspoons of garlic for 1 minute or 2, until the mixture becomes aromatic.

After another 2 minutes of cooking, stir in a quarter of a cup of fish sauce. First, add enough water to the pineapple juice so that you have a total of 8 cups, and then add the lemongrass stalk to the saucepan. Bring to a boil, then add the pineapple pieces that have been retained, mushrooms, tomatoes, and half a teaspoon of pepper. Bring the mixture back up to a boil, then reduce the heat, cover, and let it simmer for ten minutes. In the meanwhile, bring the remaining oil to a simmer in a frying pan. Add the remainder of the garlic, a sprinkle of red pepper flakes, and the 2 tablespoons of fish sauce that are still in the bottle.

Cook for 2 minutes, or until the liquid has been reduced, before adding the chicken to the pan, seasoning it with a half teaspoon of pepper, and quickly frying it until cooked through. Cook the chicken in the broth for 1 minute after stirring it in.

Vietnamese Chicken Soup with Rice

Preparation time: 10 minutes
Cook time: 25 minutes
Nutrition facts (per serving): 448 Cal (16g fat, 22g protein, 1g fiber)

It's highly recommended that you use sticky rice for this warm and porridge-like chicken soup dish. As the soup boils, the sticky rice releases a lot of creamy starches and helps produce wonderful stamina.

Ingredients (servings)
2 skinless, boneless chicken thighs
1 (4x4-inch) piece dried kombu
1 (2-inch) piece ginger, peeled, crushed
3-star anise pods, to taste
1 (2-inch) cinnamon stick
2 whole cloves
4 cups chicken stock or low-sodium chicken broth
1 cup glutinous (sticky) rice or sushi rice, rinsed
1 tablespoon (or more) fish sauce
1 teaspoon palm or light brown sugar
1 scallion, thinly sliced
1 jalapeño, thinly sliced
½ cup cilantro leaves with tender stems
¼ cup thinly sliced white onion

Preparation
In a large saucepan, over medium heat, bring the chicken, kombu, ginger, star anise, cinnamon, and cloves, together with the stock and 2 cups of

water, to a boil. Turn the heat down to a gentle simmer and continue cooking the chicken until fork tender. The chicken should now be placed on a platter. The sediments may be discarded once the broth has been strained through a fine-mesh screen into a large basin. After the broth has been returned to the saucepan, stir in the rice, fish sauce, and palm sugar. Bring to a simmer and continue cooking for another 18–20 minutes, or until the rice is extremely soft. Shred the chicken, then put it back in the soup pot and season it with extra fish sauce. The soup should be divided among dishes, and then garnished with chopped scallion, jalapeno, cilantro, and onion.

Curried Chicken Coconut Noodle Soup

Preparation time: 25 minutes
Cook time: 30 minutes
Nutrition facts (per serving): 865 Cal (40g fat, 28g protein,6g fiber)

In many Asian countries, rice sticks are a common ingredient in soups. At the Vietnamese restaurant Bo Ky on Bayard Street in New York City, I was inspired to create this dish by a flavorful soup.

Ingredients (6 servings)

2 garlic cloves, minced

2 tablespoons vegetable oil

4 tablespoons curry powder

3 cups chicken broth

2 (14 oz.) cans unsweetened coconut milk

1 cup water

2 stalks of lemongrass, the outer leaves discarded, ends trimmed, and 5 inches of the lower stalks minced

10 (⅛ inch thick) slices of peeled fresh gingerroot

1 teaspoon black peppercorns

1 whole chicken breast with skin and bones

½ lb. dried rice-stick noodles

6 tablespoons fresh lime juice

6 tablespoons Asian fish sauce, such as nuoc mam

⅓ cup chopped fresh coriander

Asian chili oil, to taste

Preparation

Garlic, oil, and curry powder are cooked together in a large pot over moderately low heat, stirring, until the garlic is aromatic, about 30 seconds. Cook for a few minutes before removing from heat and straining through a fine-mesh sieve into an airtight container. It should take around 20 minutes of poaching until the chicken is cooked thoroughly. With a slotted spoon, transfer the chicken to a basin and allow it to cool while reserving the heated poaching sauce.

In a large bowl, soak the noodles in warm water to cover for 5 minutes. Drain them and cook the noodles in a big pot of salted boiling water for 5 minutes. Using a colander, rinse the noodles in cold water before draining well. Squeeze lime juice over the poaching mixture before adding in shredded chicken and a generous amount of fish sauce. Divide the noodles among 6 to 8 bowls and pour the boiling soup over them. Cook the soup over medium heat, stirring occasionally, until hot. Incorporate the coriander and chili oil into the soup.

Authentic Oxtail Pho

Preparation time: 20 minutes

Cook time: 6 hours 5 minutes

Nutrition facts (per serving): 566 Cal (18.3g fat, 30.4g protein, 3g fiber)

This recipe for pho with oxtail is the real deal. It has always been cooked in this manner in my husband's family, and it is just delectable. This warming noodle soup has been a staple in our home for as long as my children can remember. It's at its very best on a dreary, rainy day. You may top it up with hoisin sauce and sriracha if you want.

Ingredients (8 servings)

Water, to cover

1½ lbs. beef oxtail, or to taste

2 Spanish onions, peeled, divided

1 tablespoon fish sauce, or to taste

1 tablespoon whole star anise pods

1 cinnamon stick

Salt, to taste

3 tablespoons beef pho flavor paste

2 bunches scallions, chopped

1 bunch fresh cilantro, chopped

1 (16 oz.) package dried rice noodles, or to taste

1 (12 oz.) package beef pho meatballs, halved, or to taste

½ lb. sirloin steak, thinly sliced, or to taste

1 lime, cut into 8 wedges

4 teaspoons white sugar, or to taste

1 (8 oz.) package bean sprouts

1 bunch Thai basil leaves, torn into bite-size pieces

1 (2.8 oz.) can crispy fried shallots, or to taste

Preparation

In a large saucepan, bring the oxtail and the water to a boil. Remove the froth and oil off the surface of the liquid. Include one onion, fish sauce, star anise, cinnamon, and salt in the recipe. Mix in the pho flavor paste, then cover the pot with a lid that's just partially on. Turn the heat down and let the soup boil for at least six hours. Slice the remaining onion very thinly, then cut it in half to get 2 halves. Add the scallions and cilantro to the bowl and mix well. After placing the noodles in a large dish, rinse them well.

After covering the item with warm water, let it soak for 1 hour. 20 minutes before the end of the cooking time for the broth, the meatballs should be added. Bring a tiny amount of water in a pot up to a boil. After draining the noodles, place them for a minute and a half in a pot of boiling water. Place noodles in each of the 8 big bowls. Add some sliced sirloin to the top of each bowl. Place the oxtail, meatballs, and broth in the pot. Try it out, and season it as you see fit. Squeeze the juice of 1-2 lime wedges into each bowl and combine with half a teaspoon of sugar. On top, arrange bean sprouts, shallots, and basil along with the cilantro and onion combination.

Authentic Pho

Preparation time: 20 minutes

Cook time: 8 hours

Nutrition facts (per serving): 509 Cal (11g fat, 34.5g protein,3 g fiber)

This real bowl of pho takes some time, but it's well worth the effort. The secret is in the broth, which is prepared by slowly simmering the ingredients for at least 6 hours.

Ingredients (4 servings)

5 lbs. beef marrow or knuckle bones

2 lbs. beef chuck, cut into 2 pieces

2 (3-inch) pieces ginger, halved lengthwise, lightly bruised with the flat side of a knife

2 yellow onions, peeled and charred

¼ cup fish sauce

3 oz. rock sugar (found at Asian markets) or 3 tablespoons granulated sugar

10 whole star anise, lightly toasted in a dry pan

6 whole cloves, lightly toasted in a dry pan

1 tablespoon sea salt, or to taste

Pho

1 lb. dried rice noodles (banh pho), soaked and cooked according to package instructions

⅓ lb. beef sirloin, slightly frozen, then sliced paper-thin across the grain

½ yellow onion, sliced paper thin

3 scallions, cut into thin rings

⅓ cup chopped cilantro

1 lb. bean sprouts

10 sprigs Asian basil (may substitute regular basil or mint)

1 dozen saw-leaf herb leaves (optional)

6 Thai bird chili pepper or 1 serrano chili pepper, cut into thin rings

1 lime, cut into 6 thin wedges

Freshly ground black pepper

Chili sauce, to taste (optional)

Hoisin sauce, to taste (optional)

Preparation

Bring 6 quarts (24 cups) of water to a boil in a big stock pot that you've dragged over to the heat. In the meanwhile, place the beef bones, beef chuck, and just enough water to cover them in a smaller saucepan. Bring this mixture to a boil, and then continue to simmer it for another 5 minutes. Take the saucepan from the heat and, using tongs, transfer the beef and bones to the larger pot of water that is already boiling. Discard the water that was used to cook the meat. (This results in a broth that has fewer contaminants.) When the water has reached the boiling point again, bring the heat down to a low simmer. Remove any foam that's floating on the water's surface.

After the ginger and onions have been browned, stir in the fish sauce and sugar. Simmer over low heat, scraping off any foam that forms, for around 40 minutes, or until the beef chuck is cooked. It is important to prevent the broth from reaching a rolling boil. The surface of the soup should only ever show signs of the occasional appearance of a bubble. (This lowers the likelihood that your broth will have any cloudiness.) Take 1 piece of the chuck out of the broth, place it in a basin filled with cold water, and let it sit there for 10 minutes. After that, drain the chuck, slice it very thinly, and store it in the refrigerator. Put the second piece of chuck in the broth, and then let it continue to simmer over low heat for another half an hour.

After the soup has been allowed to simmer for a total of 1 hour and 10 minutes, place the star anise and cloves inside of a spice bag or a piece of cheesecloth, and then drop the bag into the liquid. Allow the spices to soak the soup for a further half an hour until the flavor is aromatic. (A total of 2 hours will have been spent with the soup simmering.) Take out the onion and spice package, and then throw them away together. Keep the chuck in the pot and continue to boil it over low heat, scraping off any foam that forms as required, until you're ready to assemble the pho together. (The broth could have a somewhat salty flavor, but after the noodles and other toppings are added, the flavor will be more well-rounded.) After straining the broth, throw away any solids that were left behind.

Pho

Put the cooked noodles in the bowls that have been heated up. (If the noodles aren't hot anymore, dunk them for a few seconds in water that's boiling to prevent them from causing the soup to become cold.) On top of the noodles, arrange a few slices of the raw sirloin and thinly sliced beef chuck that was previously saved. Place between 2 and 3 cups of the broth in each dish (The ratio of rice noodles to broth should be somewhere around 1 to 3.). The raw beef will be cooked over a low heat in the hot broth. Add the thinly sliced onions, scallions, and cilantro to the dish as a garnish. Serve immediately, and let each diner to customize their bowl of pho by adding bean sprouts, herbs, chili peppers, lime juice, and black pepper, as desired.

Vietnamese Pho Ga Chicken

Preparation time: 15 minutes

Cook time: 46 minutes

Nutrition facts (per serving): 373 Cal (11.4 g fat, 17.7 g protein, 0.4fiber)

This is a recipe that my mother came up with many years ago when she devised a method to make Vietnamese cuisine on the go. A variety of garnishes, including as bean sprouts, Thai basil and chilies, are available. Alternatively, you may serve the noodles with the sauce recipe without the broth, which is known as kho in Vietnamese.

Ingredients (8 servings)

1 whole chicken

3 thumb-sized pieces of ginger, peeled and sliced in half vertically

5 large shallots, peeled

1 small piece of cassia bark, or 1 cinnamon stick

3-star anises

1 tablespoon coriander seeds

1 black cardamom pods, cracked open

2 tablespoons salt (plus more to parboil the chicken)

3 tablespoons fish sauce

9 cups water

Pho rice noodles, to taste

Servings

Scallions

½ onion, sliced very thinly

Freshly cracked black pepper, to taste

Birds-eye chili pepper, sliced

Lime wedges, to taste

Preparation

Fill a big enough saucepan with hot water to accommodate the chicken. Stir in some salt and chicken to the saucepan and then bring it to the boil. After a single minute of boiling, take the chicken from the pot and pour away the liquid. Dry roast the ginger and shallots until fragrant and faintly colored in a skillet over medium heat. Remove the ginger and shallots from the dish and set them aside. Reduce the temperature to medium-low. Toast the cinnamon, star anise, coriander seeds, and black cardamom pod (if using) to release their aromas. Make sure they don't catch fire. Place the spices in a spice bag.

Shred or slice the chicken while the stock is simmering. Using the box directions, make pho rice noodles. Shallots may be divided into white and green sections. The green sections should be sliced thinly while the white parts are swiftly poached in the liquid. The onion should also be sliced extremely finely. Serve with pho rice noodles, chicken, scallions, and thinly sliced onions on top. Add a generous amount of freshly ground pepper to the dish. Bring the soup back to a boil, then spoon it into dishes to serve.

Day After Thanksgiving Pho

Preparation time: 15 minutes

Cook time: 2 hours 15 minutes

Nutrition facts (per serving): 755 Cal (27.3g fat, 24g protein, 1.3 g fiber)

A Vietnamese twist on turkey noodle soup can be achieved with the addition of aromatic spices and rice noodles.

Ingredients (4 servings)

1 whole cardamom pod

2 whole cloves

1 star anise pod

1 teaspoon fennel seeds

2 teaspoons coriander seed

1 (2 inch) piece fresh ginger, peeled and smashed

½ onion, peeled, optional

1 turkey carcass

8 cups water, or more as needed

1 (16 oz.) package dried flat rice noodles

¼ cup fish sauce

Salt, to taste

1 cup shredded leftover cooked turkey

1 tablespoon shredded fresh basil leaves, optional

1 tablespoon chopped fresh cilantro, optional

¼ onion, thinly sliced, optional

1 lime, cut into wedges, optional

1 tablespoon chili-garlic sauce

Preparation

In a small pan over low heat, toast the cardamom pod, cloves, star anise, fennel, and coriander until aromatic, 5 to 7 minutes. Place the spices in the middle of a square of cheesecloth that is 8 inches by 8 inches. Using kitchen twine, bind the cheesecloth edges together. In the same skillet, cook the ginger and half the onion for approximately 3 minutes on each side, until just beginning to brown.

Over medium heat, combine the turkey carcass, ginger, onion, and sachet with the water. Bring to a boil, then lower to a simmer. Simmer for 2 hours. Over high heat, bring a large pot of lightly salted water to a rolling boil. Once the water is boiling, toss in the rice noodles, and bring to a boil. Cook the noodles uncovered, tossing regularly, until the noodles have cooked through, but are still firm to the biting, 4 to 5 minutes. Drain carefully in a colander put in the sink.

Make a soup with only the broth and add the other ingredients. Remove any meat that has fallen from the bones, if required, by straining the soup. Salt and fish sauce may be added to the mix. Divide the rice noodles and turkey meat equally into 4 big dishes. Top with the chopped basil and cilantro, and a few thinly sliced onions, if you want. Soup should be poured on top. Hot sauce and a lime wedge are optional accompaniments.

Detox Pho with Beef Mushrooms and Kale

Preparation time: 40 minutes
Cook time: 1 hour
Nutrition facts (per serving): 331 Cal (4g fat,36 g protein,5 g fiber)

This soup is a great opportunity to show off a slow-simmered, rich beef broth, or you can use a store-bought base if you're short on time. Either way, you're sure to appreciate the distinctive Vietnamese tastes of aromatic herbs and crisp vegetables. Most stores have fish sauce, which gives the soup a flavorful (but not fishy) dimension.

Ingredients (4 servings)

12 oz. beef eye of round steak

2 (2-inch) pieces of ginger, unpeeled and thinly sliced

4 garlic cloves, smashed

2-star anise pods

1 cinnamon stick

5 whole cloves

8 cups beef bone broth or store-bought low-sodium beef broth

1 teaspoon Asian fish sauce

Kosher salt, to taste

4 oz. dried rice noodles, such as vermicelli or Bahn pho (rice sticks)

8 oz. kale, stemmed and roughly chopped

4 oz. assorted mushrooms, such as cremini, shitake, oyster, beech, and/or maitake, sliced if large

Optional

1 cup mung bean sprouts

½ cup fresh herbs such as basil, mint, and/or cilantro

1 small red or green chili pepper, thinly sliced

1 scallion, thinly sliced

½ small red onion, thinly sliced and rinsed in cold water

1 small carrot, julienned

1 lime, cut into wedges

Preparation

Put the steak in the freezer to make slicing it more convenient. Heat some salted water in a medium saucepan. Stir in the ginger, garlic, star anise, cinnamon, and cloves to a large saucepan heated over medium heat. Toast the spices for approximately 3 minutes, stirring regularly until aromatic and lightly toasted. Add the broth, cover, and bring the mixture to a slow simmer.

Allow to boil for 20 minutes with a lid partly on. Remove the ginger, garlic, and other spices from the broth using a slotted spoon, spider strainer, or small sieve and throw them away. Salt and an extra ½ teaspoon fish sauce may be added to the broth after adding the fish sauce, if desired. Simmer the pho soup, covered, for at least 15 minutes. Cook the noodles according to package instructions in a medium saucepan of boiling water. Divide the noodles into 4 dishes and serve immediately. Slice the steak as thinly as possible after removing it from the freezer.

Simmer the kale and the mushrooms in the stock for 2 to 3 minutes or until tender. Sauté the thinly sliced beef for 20 to 30 seconds, or until barely cooked through (it'll continue to cook in soup). Divide the meat among the dishes using tongs. Put noodles in dishes and top with broth, greens, and mushrooms. To serve, top with any garnishes you'd like.

Detox Pho

Preparation time: 10 minutes
Cook time: 10 minutes
Nutrition facts (per serving): 330 Cal (10.1g fat, 37.2g protein, 0.3 g fiber)

This recipe, which combines tart and sweet flavors, goes well with fluffy white rice. Be careful not to overcook the squid, since this can cause it to turn rubbery.

Ingredients (4 servings)

2 tablespoons vegetable oil

3 cloves garlic, minced

1 onion, cut into wedges

2 lbs. squid, cleaned and cut into ½-inch rings

½ fresh pineapple - peeled, cored and chopped

4 stalks celery, cut into 2-inch pieces

4 tablespoons fish sauce

1 teaspoon white sugar

1 teaspoon ground black pepper

Preparation

Both the onion and the garlic should be heated in a large pan over medium-high heat. Fry the garlic until it becomes a golden-brown color. Stir-frying the onion for one minute after it has been added. Cook the squid until their white color is almost completely lost (don't overcook). The pineapple, celery, fish sauce, sugar, and pepper should all be added at this point. Cook in a wok for 2 minutes. Serve it in any beautiful dish and enjoy.

Vietnamese Style Vegetarian Curry Soup

Preparation time: 30 minutes
Cook time: 1 hour 30 minutes
Nutrition facts (per serving): 784 Cal (26.5g fat, 16.4g protein, 2g fiber)

Curry powder prepared in the manner of Vietnam may be found in Asian markets. If you're unable to get it, you may use Madras curry powder. You may transform this flavorful soup into a hearty stew by lowering the amount of water and vegetable stock by one half. Rice and French toast should be served with this dish.

Ingredients (servings)

2 tablespoons vegetable oil
1 onion, coarsely chopped
2 shallots, thinly sliced
2 cloves garlic, chopped
2-inch piece fresh ginger root, thinly sliced
1 stalk lemon grass, cut into 2-inch pieces
4 tablespoons curry powder
1 green bell pepper, coarsely chopped
2 carrots, peeled and diagonally sliced
8 mushrooms, sliced
1 oz. fried tofu, cut into bite-size pieces
4 cups vegetable broth
4 cups water

2 tablespoons vegetarian fish sauce (optional)

2 teaspoons red pepper flakes

1 bay leaf

2 makrut lime leaves

8 small potatoes, quartered

1 (14 oz.) can coconut milk

2 cups fresh bean sprouts, for garnish

8 sprigs fresh chopped cilantro, for garnish

Preparation

In a large stockpot, bring the oil to a temperature of medium heat. Onion and shallots should be cooked until they are transparent and tender. Add the curry powder, garlic, ginger, and lemon grass, and stir to combine. Cook for around 5 minutes to bring out all of the flavors that the curry has to offer. Mix in the carrots, green pepper, mushrooms, and tofu after heating through. Combine the water and vegetable stock in the pan. Add flavor by seasoning with fish sauce, crushed red pepper, bay leaf, and lime leaves. Bring to a boil, then add the potatoes along with the coconut milk and mix to combine. After the soup has returned to a boil, lower the heat and allow it to simmer for 40 to 60 minutes, or until the potatoes are fork-tender. Bean sprouts and cilantro should be piled high on top of each dish before serving.

Main Dishes

Vietnamese Style Beef Noodle Broth

Preparation time: 15 minutes
Cook time: 15 minutes
Nutrition facts (per serving): 214 Cal (6g fat, 21g protein, 1g fiber)

This one-pot dinner is topped with crispy mung bean sprouts and chopped fresh basil. Pho, a typical Vietnamese soup, served as the inspiration for this dish. On the side, you could also put lime wedges and a bottle of an Asian Chile sauce like sriracha. Another option is to serve it with both.

Ingredients (6 servings)

2 teaspoons canola oil
1 lb. beef flank steak, very thinly sliced against the grain
4 cups chopped Bok choy, (1 small head, about 1 lb.)
4 cups reduced-sodium chicken broth
1 cup water
4 oz. wide rice noodles
2 teaspoons reduced-sodium soy sauce
1 ½ cups mung bean sprouts
4 tablespoons chopped fresh basil, or to taste

Preparation

Over high heat, bring the oil to a boil in a soup pot or Dutch oven. Add the meat and cook it for approximately 2 minutes, tossing it often, until almost done. Make sure to keep the liquids in the saucepan after transferring the meat to the platter with the tongs. After adding the bok choy to the stove, boil it for approximately 2 minutes while tossing it occasionally, until it has wilted. After adding the broth and water, cover the pot and bring the mixture to a boil. After adding the noodles and soy sauce, continue to boil for approximately 4 minutes, or until the noodles are soft. After returning the meat to the saucepan, continue cooking it for an additional minute or 2 until completely warm. To serve, ladle the soup into bowls and top each with bean sprouts and basil. To be served hot.

Vietnamese Chicken and Long Grain Rice Congee

Preparation time: 10 minutes
Cook time: 2 hours
Nutrition facts (per serving): 642 Cal (42.3 g fat, 53 g protein, 1g fiber)

Soups like congee, a favorite of many Asians, go mostly unnoticed yet are filling and hearty. When you're feeling a bit under the weather, this dish is light, tasty, and simple to consume. It seems more difficult than it is. Most of the time, I simply toss stuff together, leave, then return to check whether it's ready.

Ingredients (4 servings)

⅛ cup uncooked jasmine rice
1 (2.5 lb.) whole chicken
3 (2 inch) pieces fresh ginger root
1 stalk lemongrass, chopped
1 tablespoon salt, or to taste
¼ cup chopped cilantro
⅛ cup chopped fresh chives
Ground black pepper, to taste
1 lime, cut into 8 wedges

Preparation

Prepare chicken in a large stockpot. Add water to completely submerge the chicken. Pour in the ginger, lemon grasses, and salt. Take off the heat, cover, and simmer for an hour to an hour and a half. Return the broth to the stock pot after straining it. Wait for the chicken to cool completely before dissecting it into bite-sized pieces and putting it aside. Boil the mixture, then add the rice and bring to a gentle boil. Cook, stirring periodically, for 30 minutes over medium heat. Adjust with water or extra salt as required. If you like a thicker congee, prepare it for an extra 45 minutes after the initial cooking time. Top the congee with chicken, cilantro, chives, and pepper before serving. Lime juice may be added to taste.

Banh Mi Burgers

Preparation time: 30 minutes

Cook time: 10 minutes

Nutrition facts (per serving): 487 Cal (27 g fat, 32.7g protein, 0.8g fiber)

After a trip to the farmer's market on Saturday morning, I made these burgers for a weekend dinner. To my surprise, I discovered that I had several young cucumbers in the fridge. Although they're not typical, my husband and I both loved them right away. On the cooktop, burgers may also be made. My preferred method of grilling is charcoal for a smokey finish.

Ingredients (4 servings)

2 carrots, coarsely shredded

¼ cup unseasoned rice vinegar

1 tablespoon sugar

½ cup mayonnaise

2 tablespoons Tabasco

2 teaspoons tomato paste

1 garlic clove, minced

Kosher salt and freshly ground pepper, to taste

1 ½ lbs. ground beef chuck

1 ½ teaspoons curry powder

2 tablespoons vegetable oil

2 tablespoons unsalted butter, softened

1 (24 inch) baguette, quartered crosswise and split

2 pickled jalapeños, thinly sliced
12 cilantro sprigs

Preparation

Pre-heat oven on 400°F. Toss the carrots with the rice vinegar and sugar in a small dish and let them sit for 10 minutes; drain the water. Add salt and pepper to taste. In a small dish, combine the mayonnaise with Tabasco sauce, tomato paste, and garlic; whisk until well combined. Make four 1-inch-thick oval patties using the meat, each measuring 6 inches in length. Add salt and pepper to taste, along with the curry powder. Add the oil to a big pan and bring it to a boil.

In approximately 12 minutes, cook the patties over medium heat, rotating once, until they're medium-rare. Meanwhile, butter the baguette slices on both sliced sides. To toast the bread, place it on a baking sheet with the sliced side up and bake it for approximately 5 minutes. Garnish each piece of toast with a patty, pickled shredded carrots, pickled jalapenos, and cilantro stems before spreading the Tabasco-spiked mayonnaise on top. Serve the heated sandwiches with their lids on.

Banh Mi Style Vietnamese Baguette

Preparation time: 20 minutes

Cook time: 25 minutes

Nutrition facts (per serving): 760 Cal (22.8g fat, 19.5 g protein, 0.3g fiber)

Your visitors will adore these sandwiches, and you'll love them too! Fresh, flavorful, and widely available, these ingredients will make your mouth water with marinated delight. If you don't want to use fish sauce, here's a hearty vegetarian variation of the high-calorie sandwich that uses portobello mushrooms instead of the traditional assortment of meat atop mayonnaise.

Ingredients (2 servings)

2 portobello mushroom caps, sliced

2 teaspoons olive oil

Salt and pepper, to taste

1 carrot, sliced into sticks

1 daikon (white) radish, sliced into sticks

1 cup rice vinegar

½ cup fresh lime juice

½ cup cold water

½ cup chilled lime juice

2 teaspoons soy sauce

1 teaspoon nuoc mam (Vietnamese fish sauce)

½ teaspoon toasted sesame oil

2 tablespoons canola oil

2 teaspoons minced garlic

⅓ cup white sugar

⅓ cup cold water

1 jalapeno pepper, thinly sliced

8 sprigs fresh cilantro with stems

1 medium cucumber, sliced into thin strips

2 sprigs fresh Thai basil

2 (7 inch) French bread baguettes, split lengthwise

Preparation

Pre-heat the oven to 450 degrees Fahrenheit (230 degrees C). Bake the mushrooms in a single layer on a sheet pan. Salt and pepper to taste before drizzling with a little olive oil. The oven should be preheated at 375 degrees Fahrenheit. Allow it cool for a few minutes before slicing into strips. Bring a pot of water to a boil while the mushrooms roast. In order to halt the cooking, take the carrot and radish sticks from the boiling water and put them back in the water to cool down. Pour the rice vinegar, lime juice, and water into a separate basin and mix well.

Using a slotted spoon, transfer the vegetables to a container with the vinegar and lime marinade and let them soak for at least 15 minutes, or longer if it's convenient. Salt, sugar, and water are all mixed together in a small dish with the remaining lime juice, soy sauce, and fish seasoning. Please use this as a condiment for your sandwiches.

To construct the sandwiches, spread a little amount of the sandwich sauce on both halves of the French bread. Top each roll with a bit extra sauce and the roasted mushrooms from the bottom half. Add a few slices of jalapeño, carrots, radish, cucumber, basil, and cilantro (without the marinade). Serve the sandwiches with the bread tops as a closure.

Braised Green Beans with Fried Tofu

Preparation time: 20 minutes
Cook time: 20 minutes
Nutrition facts (per serving): 380 Cal (21.6 g fat, 11.7 g protein, 0.4g fiber)

It's hard to think this meal is Vietnamese at all! Diners love it so much that even meat and potatoes fans can't get enough. Considering how delicious the sauce is, I suggest making lots of white rice to go with it!

Ingredients (4 servings)

2 tablespoons white sugar

3 tablespoons soy sauce

1 cup dry white wine

½ cup chicken broth

1 (14 oz.) package tofu, drained

Salt and pepper, to taste

1 tablespoon cornstarch

3 cups oil for frying, or as needed

1 onion, chopped

4 plum tomatoes, sliced into thin wedges

12 oz. fresh green beans, trimmed and cut into 3-inch pieces

1 cup bamboo shoots, drained and sliced

1 cup chicken broth, or as needed

2 tablespoons cornstarch

3 tablespoons water

Preparation

Mix the white sugar, soy sauce, white wine, and half a cup of chicken broth in a small bowl. Remove the sauce from the heat and set it aside. Cut the tofu into cubes and pat it dry using paper towels. Salt and pepper the cubes before serving. Cornstarch should be sprayed on both sides. In a big, deep pan set over medium-high heat, warm a little more than an inch of oil. The oil should be 375 degrees F in a deep-fryer if you have one, so fill it up to the required amount (190 degrees C). The tofu should be fried until it's golden brown on both sides and then serve. Turn a little at a time. Drain on paper towels after removing from the oil using a slotted spoon. The oil should be heated to medium-high heat in a separate skillet. For 3 to 5 minutes, sauté and stir the onions and green beans. Add salt and pepper to taste. Tomatoes should be added and cooked for approximately 4 minutes. Then, whisk in the bamboo stalks and mix well.

Braised Spiced Pork with Cao Lau Noodles

Preparation time: 20 minutes
Cook time: 10 minutes
Nutrition facts (per serving): 488 Cal (8.1g fat, 23.7g protein, 2g fiber)

This dish combines the best of both worlds: crisp, fresh ingredients combined with rich, sweet, and herbal sauces. Serve with more herbs, chili peppers, and limes so that everyone may make their own bowls to their individual tastes!

Ingredients (6 servings)

2 tablespoons soy sauce

4 cloves garlic, minced, or more to taste

2 teaspoons Chinese five-spice powder

2 teaspoons white sugar

1 teaspoon paprika

¼ teaspoon chicken bouillon granules

1 ½ lbs. pork tenderloin, cut into cubes

2 tablespoons vegetable oil

2 tablespoons water

2 lbs. fresh thick Vietnamese-style rice noodles

2 cups bean sprouts

1 cup torn lettuce leaves

1 bunch green onions, chopped

¼ cup fresh basil leaves

¼ cup fresh cilantro leaves

¼ cup crispy chow Mein noodles, or more to taste

Preparation

Soy sauce, garlic, and Chinese 5-spice are combined in a big glass or ceramic dish with sugar, paprika, and chicken bouillon. Toss in the pork chunks and coat well. Marinate in the refrigerator for at least an hour before serving. Rinse and pat dry the pork after removing it from the marinade. Rub out the remaining marinade. Using a medium-sized pan or wok, heat the oil until it shimmers and smokes. Cook and stir the pork for 4 to 7 minutes until it's browned.

Cook and stir in the remaining 2 minutes or so, until the liquid has evaporated and the pork is well cooked. Add water to a big saucepan and bring it to a boil. Using a fork, break apart the rice noodles in a bowl of cold water. Cook the noodles for 30 seconds in hot water, or until half-tender. Cook the noodles and bean sprouts together for 30 seconds longer, or until the noodles are soft but firm to the biting. Drain. In a large serving dish, combine the noodles and pork mixture. Add lettuce, green onion, basil and cilantro to the noodles before adding the crispy chow Mein.

Cao Lau Vietnamese Noodle Bowl

Preparation time: 20 minutes

Cook time: 10 minutes

Nutrition facts (per serving): 488 Cal (8.1g fat, 23.7g protein, 0.7 g fiber)

Traditionally, Cao Lau is a dish prepared with rice noodles, pork, and vegetables that is exclusively available in Hoi An, Vietnam. Easy-to-find components make this Cao Lau dish a good substitute for true Cao Lau. Rice noodles of the same thickness as linguine may be used in this recipe.

Ingredients (6 servings)

2 tablespoons soy sauce

4 cloves garlic, minced, or more to taste

2 teaspoons Chinese five-spice powder

2 teaspoons white sugar

1 teaspoon paprika

¼ teaspoon chicken bouillon granules

1 ½ lbs. pork tenderloin, cut into cubes

2 tablespoons vegetable oil

2 tablespoons water

2 lbs. fresh thick Vietnamese-style rice noodles

2 cups bean sprouts

1 cup torn lettuce leaves

1 bunch green onions, chopped

¼ cup fresh basil leaves

¼ cup fresh cilantro leaves

¼ cup crispy chow Mein noodles, or more to taste

Preparation

Soy sauce, garlic and Chinese 5-spice are combined in a big glass or ceramic dish with sugar, paprika and chicken bouillon. Toss in the pork chunks and coat well. Marinate in the refrigerator for at least an hour before serving. Rinse and pat dry the pork after removing it from the marinade. Rub out the remaining marinade. Using a medium-sized pan or wok, heat the oil until it shimmers and smokes. Cook and stir the pork for 4 to 7 minutes until it is browned.

Cook and stir in the remaining 2 minutes or so, until the liquid has evaporated and the pork is well cooked. Add the water to a big saucepan and bring it to a boil. Using a fork, break apart the rice noodles in a bowl of cold water. Cook the noodles for 30 seconds in hot water, or until half-tender. Cook the noodles and bean sprouts together for 30 seconds longer, or until the noodles are soft but firm to the biting. Drain. In a large serving dish, combine the noodles and pork mixture. Add lettuce, green onion, basil and cilantro to the noodles before adding the crispy chow Mein.

Caramel Coated Catfish

Preparation time: 15 minutes
Cook time: 30 minutes
Nutrition facts (per serving): 404 Cal (17.4 g fat, 38.8g protein, 0.1 g fiber)

Vietnamese-style catfish covered with a caramelized fish sauce and cooked in the way of the Vietnamese. Because it is rich in heart-healthy fats and retains its moisture even after being braised, catfish is an excellent option when looking for a fish to utilize for this cooking method. When the catfish is newly cooked, biting into the flesh that has been braised makes for a delightful experience since it's both firm and juicy.

Ingredients (4 servings)
⅓ cup water
2 tablespoons fish sauce
2 shallots, chopped
4 cloves garlic, minced
1 ½ teaspoon ground black pepper
¼ teaspoon red pepper flakes
⅓ cup water
⅓ cup white sugar
2 lbs. catfish fillets
½ teaspoon white sugar
1 tablespoon fresh lime juice
1 green onion, thinly sliced
½ cup chopped cilantro

Preparation

In a small dish, combine ⅓ of a cup of water with the fish sauce, then put aside. In a separate bowl, combine the shallots, garlic, black pepper, and red pepper flakes, and then put this mixture aside. In a large pan, combine ⅓ of a cup of water with ⅓ of a cup of sugar. Heat the mixture over medium heat, turning the mixture regularly, until the sugar becomes a deep golden brown. Incorporate the fish sauce combination in a careful manner, then bring to a boil. After stirring in the shallot mixture, wait for the shallots to get tender before adding the catfish to the pan.

Cover the pan and cook the catfish for about 5 minutes on each side, or until it flakes easily when tested with a fork. Put the catfish on a big platter, cover it, and put it to the side for a moment. Raise the temperature to high, then add sugar gradually while stirring it in. Mix in the juice of half a lime as well as any sauce that has accumulated on the dish. Bring to a boil and then decrease the heat to maintain a simmer for the remaining time. Top the fish with a sauce poured over it and garnish with green onions and cilantro.

Caramelized Pork Belly Thit Kho

Preparation time: 20 minutes

Cook time: 1 hour 13 minutes

Nutrition facts (per serving): 410 Cal (26.3g fat, 26.7g protein,0 g fiber)

In Vietnamese homes, this meal is eaten on a daily basis, but it's also served during the Vietnamese Lunar New Year, Tet. Longer cooking times result in more tender pork belly. Ahead of time, you'll be able to easily remove the fat that has congealed on the dish's surface. In addition, this causes the tastes to blend together a little more. Rice is a good accompaniment.

Ingredients (6 servings)

2 lbs. pork belly, trimmed

2 tablespoons white sugar

5 shallots, sliced

3 cloves garlic, chopped

3 tablespoons fish sauce

Ground black pepper, to taste

13 fluid oz. coconut water

6 hard-boiled eggs, peeled

Preparation

Layer the skin, fat, and meat of the pork belly into 1-inch-long pieces. In a large wok or saucepan, cook the sugar over medium heat until it begins to melt and caramelize, approximately 5 minutes. Add pork and turn the heat up to medium-high. For 3 to 5 minutes, cook and stir to render some of the fat from the meat.

Wok: Add shallots and garlic and cook for a few seconds. In a large bowl, combine fish sauce, black pepper, and pork; toss to coat evenly. Bring the coconut water to a boil before adding the rest of the ingredients. Simmer for approximately an hour, covered, with eggs and a low heat to ensure the pork is soft. Serve after approximately 10 minutes of resting the wok on the counter. Remove the fat from the dish's surface.

Chilled Maine Shrimp with Cabbage Peanuts

Preparation time: 5 minutes

Cook time: 30 minutes

Nutrition facts (per serving): 235 Cal (14g fat, 19 g protein, 1.2g fiber)

To spice up a summer potluck or to serve as a light dish when gathering in the heat of the summer, try this Vietnamese shrimp salad. Asian spicy chili sauce is required for this recipe. Sauces come in a variety of flavors, so you'll have to experiment to find the right one for you.

Ingredients (6 servings)

12 oz. cold cooked and peeled shrimp

½ small head Chinese or napa cabbage

20 sprigs fresh cilantro, divided

1 small head Boston lettuce

⅓ cup rice vinegar

3 tablespoons peanut oil

2 tablespoons fish sauce

2 tablespoons Asian chili sauce, such as sambal oelek or Sriracha

1 tablespoon sugar

1 teaspoon finely chopped fresh ginger

1 small carrot, peeled and shredded

½ cup roasted unsalted peanuts, coarsely chopped, divided

Preparation

Discard any shell fragments after inspecting the shrimp. The salad should be covered and refrigerated until ready to be served. You'll need about 5 to 6 cups of chopped up cabbage for this recipe. Slice the stems and leaves of 12 cilantro sprigs very thinly, and save the rest for garnish. Clean lettuce by separating and washing it. Toss the salad, keep the ingredients refrigerated until you're ready to do so.

In a small bowl, combine the vinegar, sugar, ginger, peanut oil, fish sauce, and hot sauce. The salad can be kept at room temperature for up to 2 hours, or covered and refrigerated if made ahead; let the cold dressing warm up before adding it. Preparation is key. Toss together in a large bowl with 6 tablespoons of chopped peanuts and 6 slices of cilantro just before serving. Gather the remaining lettuce leaves and place them on a serving platter or in a big, shallow bowl. Add the remaining 2 tablespoons of peanuts and 8 cilantro sprigs to the salad and top with a mound of lettuce.

Chicken Curry with Sweet Potatoes

Preparation time: 20 minutes
Cook time: 10 minutes
Nutrition facts (per serving): 257 Cal (5.4g fat, 21.7 g protein, 5.3 g fiber)

To make these quick and easy loaded baked potatoes, simply use leftover or store-bought cooked chicken and store-bought curry sauce. Substitute whatever vegetables you have in your fridge for the cauliflower in this recipe. You can also use russet potatoes in place of sweet potatoes.

Ingredients (4 servings)

4 medium sweet potatoes
½ cup any curry sauce
1 ½ cups chopped cooked cauliflower
8 oz. chopped cooked chicken, warmed
4 teaspoons chopped fresh cilantro

Preparation

Fork holes should be made in potatoes all throughout. Microwave on Medium for approximately 20 minutes, flipping once or twice to ensure even cooking (Another option is to bake the potatoes at 425 degrees Fahrenheit until cooked, which should take anywhere from 45 minutes to 1 hour.). Place the meat on a clean cutting board, and allow it to slightly cool before proceeding. Make a cut down the length of the potato to open it, but stop short of cutting all the way through. This will protect your hands. Hold the potatoes in a kitchen towel. Pinch the ends so that the skin is exposed. On top of each potato, spoon some curry sauce, then sprinkle on some chicken, cauliflower, and cilantro. Finally, serve hot.

Vietnamese Spring Roll with Pork and Prawns (Goi Cuon)

Preparation time: 45 minutes

Cook time: 10 minutes

Nutrition facts (per serving): 328 Cal (2 g fat, 19.6 g protein, 0.6 g fiber)

This time-honored munchie goes by a few different names, including spring roll, salad roll, fresh roll, and Vietnamese roll. No matter what you want to name it, it's one of my favorite foods to eat since it isn't only tasty but also healthful. Hoisin sauce or nuoc cham, a Vietnamese dipping sauce, may be served with the spring rolls.

Ingredients (6 servings)

½-lb. pork tenderloin, cut into thin strips

½-lb. prawns, peeled and deveined

¼-lb. rice vermicelli noodles

1 (12 oz.) package rice wrappers (such as Blue Dragon®)

1 bunch fresh cilantro, leaves picked from stems

5 spring onions, cut in half

¼ cup fresh mint leaves, or more to taste

¼ head romaine lettuce, cut into bite-size pieces

Preparation

To cook the pork, put it in a medium-sized saucepan along with some sugar and a little bit of salt. To ensure that the pork is completely soaked, add more water as necessary. Bring the water to a boil, and after it's boiling, reduce the heat to medium. Bring the pork to a boil and continue boiling for 30 minutes, or until it floats and a chopstick poked into the flesh does not produce any pink liquid. After allowing the meat to cool, take it from the bone and slice it into extremely thin slices.

To prepare the prawns, bring a big saucepan of water to a boil, then add a pinch of salt and the lemongrass to the pot. After adding the prawns and bringing the water back up to a boil, decrease the heat to a low setting and continue to simmer for approximately 1 to 2 minutes, or until they're opaque. After turning off the heat, let the prawns and the liquid used for poaching come to room temperature together. Prepare the vermicelli in accordance with the instructions that are printed on the package. After adding vermicelli to water that was already boiling, I let it cook for about 4 to 5 minutes, or until tender but still has some bite to it. Drain completely after stopping the cooking process by rinsing in cold water.

Warm water should be placed in a big, shallow dish. Put one sheet of rice paper into the warm water, and let it soak there for 10 to 15 seconds, or until it begins to become flexible but still maintains its structure. Move to the surface where you'll be rolling. Place a ripped leaf of lettuce on the rice paper about a third of the way up from the bottom. Cucumber and carrot should be placed on top. On top of the vermicelli, place several slices of pork, then finish with more vermicelli. Garnish with chives and herbs that have been torn. Arrange 3 to 4 prawn halves in a line along the middle of the rice paper. Start rolling, and as you go, tuck in the sides of the roll like a burrito. Repeat the process until all of the ingredients have been used up and then place the finished rolls on a serving plate.

Grilled Shrimp Rice Noodle Bowl

Preparation time: 25 minutes
Cook time: 10 minutes
Nutrition facts (per serving): 565 Cal (21.3 g fat,10 g protein, 4.4 g fiber)

Try this bowl of rice noodles prepared in the manner of Vietnam. After they're cooked, the noodles will likely get clumpy and cling together. Andrea Nguyen, the creator of the recipe, came up with a brilliant solution to the problem of excessive sticking: In order for the noodles to drape over something, invert a small dish and place it at the bottom of the colander. The lime juice and mint provide a refreshing counterpoint to the sauce's mild sweetness.

Ingredients (2 servings)

5 oz. uncooked rice vermicelli noodles

½ cup lukewarm water

3 tablespoons granulated sugar

¼ cup fresh lime juice

1 tablespoon rice vinegar

5 teaspoons fish sauce (such as Three Crabs)

2 serrano chiles, thinly sliced

4 cups (¼-inch) slices green leaf lettuce

3 cups diagonally cut slices of seeded pickling cucumber

¼ cup cilantro leaves

¼ cup torn Thai basil leaves

¼ cup torn mint leaves

2 teaspoons cornstarch

1 teaspoon dark brown sugar

¼ teaspoon salt

¾ teaspoon white pepper

1-lb. large shrimp, peeled and deveined

2 tablespoons canola oil, divided

⅓ cup (¼-inch) slices green onions

3 garlic cloves, finely chopped

½ cup unsalted, dry-roasted peanuts, coarsely chopped

Preparation

Cook the rice vermicelli noodles in accordance with the instructions on the package. After draining, rinse the drain with cold water, and then drain again. In a medium bowl, combine half a cup of lukewarm water with the granulated sugar. Stir the mixture until the sugar is dissolved. Lime juice, vinegar, fish sauce, and chilies should be added, and then the mixture should be left away. Mix the lettuce, cucumber, and herbs together, then put the mixture aside.

In a large bowl, whisk together the cornstarch, brown sugar, salt, and pepper until the ingredients are well incorporated. Add the shrimp; toss to coat. Prepare a high heat in either a wok or a big skillet. To coat, add 1 and a ½ tablespoons of oil, and stir to combine. After adding half of the shrimp, sauté them for 1 minute and a half on each side, or until they have a nice sear. Take away from the heat. To the wok, add 1 and a ½ teaspoons of oil, and then continue the process with the remaining shrimp. Bring the temperature down to medium-high.

Stirring constantly, add the remaining 1 tablespoon of oil to the pan. Stir-fry the onions and garlic for thirty seconds after adding them. Bring the shrimp back into the pan and stir-fry for one minute. Step 5 Distribute about 1 cup of the lettuce mixture among the 4 big dishes. Top each meal with approximately 1 cup of the noodles and 2 teaspoons of the chopped peanuts. Distribute the shrimp in an equal amount to each dish, then top each with a quarter cup of the sauce.

Lemon Grass and Chicken Summer Rolls

Preparation time: 1 hour
Cook time: 20 minutes
Nutrition facts (per serving): 137 Cal (6.9g fat, 12.4g protein, 1.7 g fiber)

These are basically bite-sized bundles of chicken salad, wrapped in rice paper, and they are quite wonderful. They're very scrumptious and the ideal treat for when the weather is warm.

Ingredients (12 servings)
2 chicken breasts
3 stalks lemongrass
12 sheets rice paper wrappers
4 oz. rice vermicelli noodles
3 cups water
1 teaspoon chili flakes
2 cloves garlic
1 cucumber
4 tablespoons hoisin sauce
5 tablespoons creamy peanut butter
1 tablespoon lemon juice
1 tablespoon sesame oil
1 teaspoon sugar
1 tablespoon sesame seed
2 romaine hearts

1 teaspoon cilantro

1 teaspoon Thai basil

Salt, to taste

Preparation

Cut 2 lemongrass stalks into 1-inch pieces and lb. them. The chicken is added to a saucepan with water, a pinch of salt, some chili peppers, a clove of garlic, and a sprig of lemongrass. Begin heating. Then lower the temperature. Cook the chicken for 20 minutes in a covered pot without the lid. Take the chicken out of the saucepan and set it aside. Remove from the heat and let it cool for a few minutes.

The seeds should be removed and the cucumber should be sliced into thin sticks after it has been quartered. The remaining lemongrass should be minced very finely. In a food processor, combine the hoisin sauce, peanut butter, remaining garlic, water, lemon juice, sesame oil, and sugar. While you're waiting, prepare the pasta according to the directions on the box. Place in a large bowl after draining and rinsing with cold water.

Using a pair of kitchen scissors, roughly cut the noodles. Cucumber sticks, sesame seeds, and lemongrass, diced, go into the mix now. A pinch of salt will go a long way. Thinly slice the chicken. A shallow bowl or deep plate should be filled with some warm water.

After about 10 to 15 seconds, remove 1 rice paper wrapper from the water to a cutting board. Rice paper wrappers may be made by stuffing a lettuce leaf, some chicken, coriander and basil into the center. Add roughly 2 teaspoons of the noodle and cucumber mixture to the top of each serving. Now seal the log by folding in the edges and rolling it up. Keep doing this until all of your components are used. To keep the summer rolls from drying out, cover them with a moist dish towel. Make a peanut sauce to accompany the chicken summer rolls and serve immediately. Enjoy!

Maho Vietnamese Chicken

Preparation time: 15 minutes
Cook time: 20 minutes
Nutrition facts (per serving): 693 Cal (22,2g fat, 31.4g protein, 2.9 g fiber)

Simple and low-cost Vietnamese chicken dish called Maho is provided here. The fact that we regularly consume it and that my child enjoys it confirms its high quality. The finest, most affordable, and most straightforward dish for you is Classic Maho, Vietnamese Chicken Recipe. In addition, the recipe is simple to follow. Vietnamese garlic chicken is a popular dish in the country, and children like it as well, so you can be sure it's delicious. This recipe is simple to create at home and doesn't need any special equipment. You can make your own Vietnamese honey lemongrass chicken with this simple recipe.

Ingredients (4 servings)
2 cups of uncooked white rice
4 cups of fresh water
3 tablespoons of vegetable oil
2 cloves of garlic, fully minced
3 skinless, boneless chicken breast halves – cut them into bite-size equal pieces
2 tablespoons of the soy sauce, or just to taste
Half cup of the dry-roasted, unsalted peanuts
4 large size leaves of iceberg lettuce
One can of mandarin oranges, fully drained

Preparation

To begin, cook the water and rice in a standard saucepan over high heat until the rice is just about to become tender but not quite. Reduce the heat to medium-low, cover the pot tightly, and cook the rice for about 20 to 25 minutes, or until the liquid has been absorbed. Finally, you may leave the rice covered while you finish your meal. Cook and stir garlic for about a minute after it has been infused with oil in a basic skillet over medium heat.

Cook and stir the chicken for about 5 minutes, until it has seared and is starting to color gently. It's possible to extend the cooking time by adding a little soy sauce along with the peanuts, which you may do for an additional five minutes while stirring. Finally, the chicken combination must be taken off the fire. Just one cup of cooked rice should be scooped onto each of the 4 lettuce leaves. The chicken-peanut combination and mandarin orange slices must be added to the top of each dish.

Mom's Catfish in Claypot

Preparation time: 10 minutes
Cook time: 5 minutes
Nutrition facts (per serving): 212 Cal (9.8g fat, 7.9g protein, 0 g fiber)

If you're fortunate enough to be invited to a traditional Vietnamese dinner, there's a good possibility that you'll be served this ca kho to as an appetizer. Due to the fact that it's so fundamental and well-liked, it's popular in many houses, including mine, almost every other day.

Ingredients (3servings)
3 tablespoons vegetable oil
2 cloves garlic, minced
2 shallots, chopped
1-lb. fresh catfish fillet, cut in thirds
4 tablespoons caramel sauce
3 tablespoons fish sauce
3 tablespoons unsalted chicken stock or water
2 green onions, thinly sliced
½ teaspoon ground black pepper

Preparation
A clay pot or a medium-sized fry pan with moderate heat should be used to heat the vegetable oil. To make the dish, add the chopped garlic and shallots. After approximately 2 to 3 minutes of stirring, during which time the mixture should become aromatic, add the catfish pieces. Approximately 2 minutes of cooking time should be sufficient to achieve this. After adding the caramel sauce, continue to stir the fish over low

heat for one more minute, until the sauce has been absorbed by the fish. Reduce the heat, then stir in the fish sauce and the chicken stock. Simmer uncovered for 12 to 15 minutes, or until the sauce has developed a mild caramelization. Take the clay pot from the fire and serve the food directly from it. Green onions and freshly ground black pepper should be sprinkled on top.

Pasta with Vietnamese Pesto

Preparation time: 30 minutes

Cook time: 5 minutes

Nutrition facts (per serving): 694 Cal (29.8 g fat,6.8 g protein,1.4 g fiber)

It just requires one pan and one dish, pasta with pesto is one of my go-to dinner options. This is a really delicious pesto. In the event that you're unable to get fresh lemongrass, you may substitute an equivalent quantity of grated lemon zest.

Ingredients (4 servings)

1 lb. dried rice noodles

1 ½ cups chopped fresh cilantro

½ cup sweet Thai basil

2 cloves garlic, halved

½ teaspoon minced lemongrass bulb

1 jalapeno pepper, seeded and minced

1 tablespoon vegetarian fish sauce

4 tablespoons chopped, unsalted dry-roasted peanuts

7 tablespoons canola oil

½ lime, cut into wedges

Salt and pepper, to taste

Preparation

Put the rice noodles in a big bowl and cover it with cold water. Let it sit for half an hour. After draining them, place the noodles to the side. Combine the chopped cilantro, basil, garlic cloves, lemongrass, jalapeño peppers, imitation fish sauce or salt, and 2 tablespoons of the peanuts in a blender or food processor. Turn the blades of the food processor until the herbs and peanuts are roughly chopped.

While the machine is operating, a very little trickle of oil should be added. After that, the rest of the peanuts should be added, and the machine should be operated in short bursts so that the peanuts may be roughly chopped. Put the rice noodles that have been soaking in water into a big pan and add half a cup of water. Heat the skillet over medium-high heat. Continue stirring the mixture until the noodles are completely soft and the majority of the water has been absorbed.

After giving it a good toss, add nearly all of the pesto to the bowl. If the pesto is clumping together, add a few tablespoons of water. After tasting the pasta, you may adjust the flavor by adding additional of the following: pesto, lime juice, imitation fish sauce, salt, or pepper. Add the remaining 2 tablespoons of peanuts as a garnish to the spaghetti, and then serve it as soon as possible.

Roasted Brussels Sprouts

Preparation time: 30 minutes
Cook time: 1 hours
Nutrition facts (per serving): 159 Cal (9g fat, 5g protein, 5g fiber)

One of the most popular side dishes is Brussels sprouts that have been deep-fried. They retain their nutty richness and attractively browned, crisp surface while being cooked in a hot oven, which is simpler for the home chef. Rice Krispies, which are used in place of Indian puffed rice, which is harder to locate, provide crunch, and sous-chef Tien Ho's Vietnamese-style sauce offers the sprouts an unexpected depth.

Ingredients (6 servings)
1 ½ lbs. Brussels sprouts
3 tablespoons good olive oil
¾ teaspoon kosher salt
½ teaspoon freshly ground black pepper

Preparation
Turn the temperature in the oven up to 400 degrees F. Remove the brown ends from the Brussels sprouts and remove any yellow leaves or outer layers that may be present. Combine all of the ingredients in a bowl, adding in the olive oil, salt, and pepper. Place them on a baking sheet and roast them for thirty-five to forty minutes, or until they are crisp on the exterior and soft on the inside. To ensure that the sprouts brown in a concise manner, shake the pan at regular intervals. Sprinkle with more kosher salt (I prefer my fries salty, similar to how French fries are), and serve right away.

Roasted Pork Banh Mi Vietnamese Sandwich

Preparation time: 25 minutes
Cook time: 7 minutes
Nutrition facts (per serving): 263 Cal (75.9g fat, 52.2g protein, 5 g fiber)

My first true bánh m will always have a special place in my heart. When I initially tasted this sandwich, I said to myself, "This isn't simply one of the greatest." It was one of the finest meals I've ever eaten, period. The contrast in temperature between the crisp, warm meat-filled bun and the chilly, crunchy veggies adds an extra layer of enjoyment to this dish.

Ingredients (1 servings)
¼ cup julienned (2-inch matchsticks) daikon radish
¼ cup julienned (2-inch matchsticks) carrots
1 tablespoon seasoned rice vinegar
¼ cup mayonnaise
1 teaspoon hoisin sauce, or to taste
1 teaspoon sriracha hot sauce, or more to taste
1 crusty French sandwich roll
4 oz. cooked pork roast, thinly sliced
2 oz. smooth pate, thinly sliced
6 thin spears English cucumber, diced
6 thin slices jalapeno pepper, or more to taste
¼ cup cilantro leaves

Preparation

Pre-heat oven to 400 degrees Fahrenheit. Aluminum foil may be used to cover a baking pan. Sliced daikon and carrots should be coated well in seasoned rice vinegar before being served. Allow it settle for 15 to 20 minutes, or until vegetables are limp to the touch. Drain and chill, or store in the freezer. In a small bowl, combine the mayonnaise, hoisin sauce, and sriracha.

Open the French roll like a book by slicing it just enough. Pull away a little of the top half of the bread if you'd like to make room for the filling. The mayo mixture should be generously applied to the roll's internal surfaces. Transfer the cut side of the roll on the baking sheet. Bake in a preheated oven for approximately 7 minutes, until the edges begin to brown and the crust is crispy. A roll with sliced pork and pate on top of a lettuce leaf and a sprinkling of cilantro is ready to eat. To serve, slice in half.

Salt and Pepper Tofu

Preparation time: 15 minutes
Cook time: 20 minutes
Nutrition facts (per serving): 254 Cal (13 g fat,16 g protein, 6g fiber)

Dau Hu Rang Muoi Luke Nguyen revealed that "This meal reminds me of a vegetarian take on salt and pepper squid, and I really love both its ease of preparation and its varied textures."

Ingredients (4 servings)

14 oz. pack firm tofu

2 tablespoon corn flour

1 teaspoon Sichuan or black peppercorns (or a mixture of the two), ground to a powder

2 tablespoons sunflower or vegetable oil

2 red peppers, sliced

¼ broccoli head, cut into very small florets

3 ½ oz. beansprouts

2 teaspoon low-sodium soy sauce

Sesame oil, for drizzling

Handful of coriander leaves, to taste

Preparation

After draining the tofu, place it on a platter and cover it loosely in kitchen paper. Place a cutting board on the very top. If the cutting board you're using is on the lighter side, consider adding some cans to it to make it more stable; however, a cutting board that's on the heavier side should be OK on its own. Allow the cloth to sit for 10 to 20 minutes, or until it feels damp from the surplus liquid. When the tofu has been cooked, pressing it in this manner helps to give it a firmer consistency. To make the tofu seem more like a book, cut it in half along the middle. In the same manner that you would cut a piece of toast into 4 triangles, slice each piece into 8 triangles. This will give you a total of 16 pieces.

On a dish, combine the corn flour, the crushed pepper, and the 1 teaspoon of flaky sea salt. To coat the tofu, gently toss each piece in the corn flour mixture and flip it over. Warm up 1 tablespoon of oil in a wok. Cook the peppers and broccoli in a stir-fry for a few minutes, in order to slightly soften them. The bean sprouts and the soy sauce should both be added. Continue cooking for an additional 1 to 2 minutes, checking to see that the vegetables maintain their crispiness. Sprinkle with a touch of toasted sesame oil.

To make the tofu crispy, heat the remaining sunflower oil in a big nonstick frying pan and cook the tofu that has been coated for 5 minutes on each side. Place on top of the veggies and sprinkle with the chopped coriander before serving.

French-Vietnamese Shaking Beef (Bo Luc Lac)

Preparation time: 30 minutes

Cook time: 1 hour

Nutrition facts (per serving): 293 Cal (17.4g fat,21.7 g protein,2 g fiber)

Bo Luc Lac "French-Vietnamese Shaking Beef" is a beef stir fry with a French influence and a distinct Vietnamese flavor.

Ingredients (6 servings)

2 tablespoons minced garlic

2 tablespoons oyster sauce

1½ tablespoons white sugar

1 tablespoon fish sauce

1 tablespoon sesame oil

1 tablespoon soy sauce

1 teaspoon hoisin sauce

1½ lbs. beef top sirloin, cut into 1-inch cubes

Vinaigrette

½ cup rice vinegar

1½ tablespoons white sugar

1½ teaspoons salt

1 red onion, thinly sliced

Dipping Sauce

1 lime, juiced

½ teaspoon salt

½ teaspoon ground black pepper

2 tablespoons cooking oil

2 bunches watercress, torn

2 tomatoes, thinly sliced

Preparation

In a bowl, combine the beef with the garlic, oyster sauce, fish sauce, hoisin sauce, sesame oil, and hoisin sauce. 1 and a ½ teaspoons of sugar should also be included. At a minimum of an hour, meat should be marinated in the refrigerator. In a bowl, make a vinaigrette by combining the vinegar, 1 and ½ tablespoons of sugar, and 1 and a ½ teaspoons of salt. After the mixture is smooth, stir in the onion. Put the onion in the refrigerator for 10 minutes to pickle it. Lime juice, half of a teaspoon of salt, and black pepper should be mixed together in a dish until they form a smooth dipping sauce.

Place some of the dipping sauce in each of the ramekins. Once the frying oil in a wok or big pan has reached the smoking point after being heated over high heat, add the meat. About 2 minutes should be spent cooking the steak in a single layer until it's browned. Cook while stirring (or "shaking") for 2 to 4 minutes, depending on the desired degree of doneness for the meat. A serving dish should be covered with watercress, and then tomatoes should be placed on top. Vinaigrette should be drizzled over tomatoes, then meat should be layered atop watercress, and onion should be placed on top. The dipping sauce should be served on the side.

Vietnamese Pulled Chicken

Preparation time: 3 hours
Cook time: 30 minutes
Nutrition facts (per serving): 157 Cal (3g fat, 24g protein, 1g fiber)

Coming up on a busy week, huh? On Sunday, use your slow cooker to make these simple poached chicken breasts flavored with the tastes of the ubiquitous Vietnamese sauce nuoc cham. The chicken breasts should be poached in chicken broth. Then, in the following days, you can eat the leftover chicken in three different ways: piled with veggies on a sandwich; combined with mayonnaise to form a creamy chicken salad; and ladled with the broth over rice noodles.

Ingredients (12 servings)

3 cups low-sodium chicken broth

3 shallots, very thinly sliced

¼ cup fish sauce

2 tablespoons packed light brown sugar

2-4 Thai chiles, very thinly sliced

1 teaspoon crushed red pepper

2 teaspoons lime zest

4 lbs. skin-on, bone-in chicken breasts

2 cups julienned or grated carrots

½ cup lime juice

⅓ cup sliced fresh mint

⅓ cup sliced fresh basil

Preparation

In a slow cooker with a capacity of 6 quarts, combine the chicken broth, shallots, fish sauce, brown sugar, chilies (or crushed red pepper), and lime zest. Place the chicken pieces, flesh side down, into the liquid. Prepare the food by either simmering it on High for 3 hours or Low for 6 hours. Place the chicken on a chopping board that has been well cleaned.

To prepare the meat, first remove the skin and then shred it. Place the chicken back into the slow cooker, then add the carrots, lime juice, mint, and basil and mix everything together.

Steamed Whole Fish with Ginger Scallions and Soy

Preparation time: 15 minutes
Cook time: 35 minutes
Nutrition facts (per serving): 212 Cal (15g fat, 18.9g protein, 1.5g fiber)

Even though it's a straightforward method, preparing entire fish in this manner is a skill that's seldom seen in Western kitchens. A fish that has been steamed to perfection is believed to be a measure of a good chef in the Vietnamese culture; those who are unable to prepare the dish correctly are seen as incompetent chefs. The flesh of a fish that has been steamed to perfection is only cooked through to the point where it meets the bone and is never dry.

Ingredients (4 servings)
1 ½-lb. whole white fish (such as sea bass, branzino, or flounder), cleaned with head and tail intact
Kosher salt and freshly ground black pepper, to taste
2 (½-inch) piece fresh ginger, peeled and finely julienned
¼ cup light soy sauce
1 tablespoon rice wine
1 scallion, white and light green parts only, julienned
4 cilantro sprigs
½ cup canola oil

Preparation

After being washed in cold water, the fish should be dried off with paper towels. Salt and pepper should be applied to the interior and outside of the fish. Put the fish on a heat-resistant plate that is both big enough to hold it (a glass pie plate works well for this) and small enough to fit inside the steamer. If the fish is too long, you may need to bend it slightly to make it fit. Place one-half of the ginger within the fish's cavity, then distribute the remaining ginger over the top of the fish.

Put some water in a wok or stockpot, then put a steamer in the wok or on the lip of the stockpot to get the water going. Be certain that the water doesn't reach the base of the steamer at any point. Over high heat, the water should be brought to a boil. Put the plate on which the fish is sitting into the steamer, cover it, and steam the fish for approximately 8 minutes, or until it flakes easily when tested with the point of a knife. During the time that the fish is being steamed, combine the soy sauce, wine, and 1 tablespoon of water in a small dish and mix to combine. Set aside.

After the fish has finished cooking, remove the dish from the steamer with care and discard any liquid that has gathered on it. The onion and the cilantro should be arranged in a row along the top of the fish. To prepare the oil for cooking, place it in a small sauté pan and heat it over high heat until it is hot but not smoking. Take the oil off the heat and pour it immediately over the scallion and cilantro to "cook" them. This will accomplish the same thing as sautéing them. After drizzling the soy sauce over the fish, serve it as soon as possible.

Spicy Green Beans

Preparation time: 15 minutes
Cook time: 15 minutes
Nutrition facts (per serving): 64 Cal (0.8 g fat, 4.1 g protein, 0.3 g fiber)

Growing up, this was always one of my go-to options for a side dish. You won't be able to eat just one serving since there's so much flavor packed into each bite! This meal, which is derived from a recipe written by Grace Young and published in "Stir-Fry to the Sky's Edge," calls for the green beans to maintain their crisp texture.

Ingredients (4 servings)

1-lb. green beans, trimmed
Salt, to taste
1 tablespoon soy sauce, low-sodium, to taste
1 tablespoon Chinese rice wine or dry sherry
1 tablespoon minced garlic
1 tablespoon minced fresh ginger
¼ teaspoon red pepper flakes
1 tablespoon peanut oil or canola oil

Preparation

Green beans should be cooked in salted water that has been brought to a boil in a saucepan beforehand. After boiling for 1 minute, remove from the heat, drain, and rinse under running cold water; thereafter, spread out on a kitchen towel to dry completely (You won't be able to stir-fry the veggies if they aren't dry before you add them to the hot wok or pan because they would instead sputter and braise.).

Position such that it's easily accessible to your wok or pan. Put the soy sauce, wine or sherry in a measuring cup or a small dish, and put it within easy reach of your wok or pan. Add the garlic, ginger, and crushed red pepper flakes into a separate small container and place it next to the stove. When using a wok with a flat bottom of 14 inches or a skillet measuring 12 inches, heat the pan over high heat until a drop of water poured to the pan evaporates within a second or 2.

Add the oil to the edges of the pan and then move the pan in a circular motion to incorporate the oil. After stirring-frying the garlic and ginger for no more than 10 seconds, add the green beans to the pan and continue cooking. After giving everything a quick toss, add the soy sauce and sherry and stir-fry everything for 1 to 2 minutes, or until the beans reach the desired crisp-tender consistency. Take it off the heat, and then serve it.

Thai Chicken Spring Rolls

Preparation time: 40 minutes

Cook time: 5 minutes

Nutrition facts (per serving): 595 Cal (30.5 g fat, 46.5 g protein, 1.4 g fiber)

Thai tastes have been incorporated into this traditional Vietnamese meal. These spring rolls are perfect for serving as an appetizer or as a lighter main course option. Wrappers that are soft and transparent provide a lovely contrast to the crisp colors and textures of the veggies.

Ingredients (4 servings)

1 cup peanut sauce

1 (1 ½ inch) piece fresh ginger root, minced

2 cloves garlic, minced

1 teaspoon soy sauce

1 lb. skinless, boneless chicken breast halves - cut into 1-inch pieces

1 teaspoon peanut oil

6 oz. fresh snow pea pods

12 oz. bean sprouts

4 green onions, chopped

1 lb. watercress, chopped

¼ cup chopped fresh cilantro

2 large carrots, peeled

1 teaspoon peanut oil

1 teaspoon soy sauce

12 spring roll wrappers

½ cup peanut sauce

Preparation

In a bowl, combine 1 cup of peanut sauce, 1 teaspoon each of ginger and garlic, and 1 tablespoon of soy sauce. After adding the chicken, continue mixing until the chicken is completely covered. After 30 minutes, transfer to the refrigerator to finish marinating. In a wok or pan, bring 1 teaspoon of peanut oil up to temperature over medium heat.

Snow peas, bean sprouts, and green onion should be cooked in the oil for 3 to 4 minutes, or until heated through but still retain their crisp texture. Move the mixture to a big bowl. Combine the watercress and the cilantro in a mixing bowl. Make thin ribbons of carrot by peeling it with a vegetable peeler and adding it to the watercress mixture. Toss the watercress mixture to evenly distribute the soy sauce that has been drizzled in.

Prepare the wok or pan by heating 1 teaspoon of oil in it. About 10 minutes into the cooking process, the chicken should no longer be pink on the interior. Warm water should be added to a big dish. Wrappers should be submerged in water for approximately 2 seconds at a time, one at a time. As each wrapper is taken from the water, fill it with 2 big spoonfuls and a small handful of the chicken and watercress mixture respectively.

When you get to the filling, fold in 2 opposing ends of the wrapper to meet it. The next step is to roll the finished product after first folding the bottom of the wrapper over the top of the filling. To serve as a dipping sauce, add a half cup of peanut sauce.

Thit Bo Xao Dau

Preparation time: 10 minutes
Cook time: 20 minutes
Nutrition facts (per serving): 376 Cal (28.6 g fat, 23.1g protein, 1.2 g fiber)

This excellent Vietnamese stir fry recipe has beef and green beans and was inspired by the cuisine of Vietnam. Place on top of warm rice.

Ingredients (4 servings)
1 clove garlic, minced
¼ teaspoon ground black pepper
1 teaspoon cornstarch
1 teaspoon vegetable oil
1 lb. sirloin tips, thinly sliced
3 tablespoons vegetable oil
½ onion, thinly sliced
2 cups fresh green beans, washed and trimmed
¼ cup chicken broth
1 teaspoon soy sauce

Preparation
Garlic, ground black pepper, cornstarch, and 1 teaspoon of vegetable oil should be mixed together in a large mixing dish. Add the meat and stir thoroughly. 1 minute should be spent heating up 2 teaspoons of oil in a big wok set to high heat. After adding the meat, continue to heat and stir it for around 2 minutes, or until the steak starts to brown. Move the meat to a big bowl and then put it to the side for later.

In the pan, heat the remaining 1 tablespoon of oil. Add the onion, and continue to cook and toss it until it is soft. Blend in the green beans and then pour in the broth. Turn the heat down to medium and cover the pan. Simmer for 4 to 5 minutes, or until the beans reach the desired consistency of delicate crispness. Mix in the soy sauce as well as the meat. Cook while stirring continuously for 1 to 2 minutes, or until the food is completely warmed through.

Vegetable Satay

Preparation time: 1 hour 30 minutes
Cook time: 30 minutes
Nutrition facts (per serving): 33 Cal (2g fat, 2g protein, g1 fiber)

This Indonesian-style satay may be prepared using fresh broccoli and cauliflower florets rather than the strips of chicken or beef that are often used in its preparation. If you want the taste of curry but without the heat, use ordinary curry powder instead of Hot Madras curry. Hot Madras curry adds a bit of a kick to it. Look in the vegetable area of your grocery store or at the salad bar for broccoli and cauliflower that has already been sliced into florets. This will save you a lot of time.

Ingredients (1 servings)

10 oz. broccoli florets
10 oz. cauliflower florets
1 tablespoon soy sauce, reduced-sodium
1 tablespoon rice vinegar
1 tablespoon toasted sesame oil
1 tablespoon fresh ginger, or ginger juice; minced
1 tablespoon peanut butter, smooth natural
1 clove garlic, minced
1 teaspoon hot curry powder
¼ teaspoon salt

Preparation

Put a big pot full of water over high heat and bring it to a boil. After adding the broccoli and cauliflower, simmer for approximately 3 minutes, or until the vegetables are crisp-tender. Drain, then rinse well under lukewarm water. In a large bowl, use a whisk to combine the soy sauce, vinegar, oil, ginger (or ginger juice), peanut butter, garlic, and curry powder until the mixture is smooth. After adding the florets, give everything a little toss to coat it. Marinate for at least 2 hours at room temperature, or cover and store in the refrigerator for up to a day in advance. To serve, skewer 2 pieces of broccoli and 2 pieces of cauliflower, alternating between them (Reserve marinade.).

Spread the marinade over the skewers once they've been arranged in a single layer on the plate.

Vermicelli Noodle Bowl

Preparation time: 35 minutes

Cook time: 25 minutes

Nutrition facts (per serving): 656 Cal (12.8g fat, 26.2g protein, 6 g fiber)

There are a lot of Vietnamese dishes that are great for when it's really hot outside. This straightforward noodle salad has grilled shrimp as the garnish and incorporates fresh herbs, rice vermicelli, cucumber, bean sprouts, and other ingredients. It's a quick and easy dish that's topped with a sweet and sour sauce that has a nice tang to it.

Ingredients (2 servings)

¼ cup white vinegar

¼ cup fish sauce

2 tablespoons white sugar

2 tablespoons lime juice

1 clove garlic, minced

¼ teaspoon red pepper flakes

½ teaspoon canola oil

2 tablespoons chopped shallots

2 skewers

8 medium shrimp, with shells

1 (8 oz.) package rice vermicelli noodles

1 cup finely chopped lettuce

1 cup bean sprouts

1 English cucumber, cut into 2-inch matchsticks

¼ cup finely chopped pickled carrots

¼ cup finely chopped daikon radish

3 tablespoons chopped cilantro

3 tablespoons finely chopped Thai basil

3 tablespoons chopped, fresh mint

¼ cup crushed peanuts

Preparation

In a small bowl, combine the sugar, vinegar, fish sauce, lime juice, garlic, and red pepper flakes by whisking the ingredients together. Put the sauce in a separate bowl. Heat vegetable oil a small pan over medium heat. After adding the shallots, continue to heat and stir them for around 8 minutes until they have become pliable and gently caramelized.

Prepare an outside grill with a medium heat setting and grease the grate just a little bit. Place four shrimp on each skewer, then grill them for 1 to 2 minutes on each side, or until the shrimp become pink and are charred on the exterior. Set aside. Start the boiling process with a big saucepan of water. After 12 minutes, add the vermicelli noodles and continue to simmer until they have softened. After rinsing the noodles in cold water and separating them with a swirling motion, drain them.

Assemble the vermicelli bowls by arranging the cooked noodles in one half of each serving dish, then the lettuce and bean sprouts in the other half of each bowl. Cucumbers, carrots, daikon, cilantro, Thai basil, mint, peanuts, and caramelized shallots should be arranged on top of each dish before serving. Place the shrimp skewers on top of the dish, then pass the sauce on the side. Before eating, pour the sauce over the top and mix everything well to coat it.

Vietnamese Aromatic Lamb Chops

Preparation time: 10 minutes
Cook time: 20 minutes
Nutrition facts (per serving): 555 Cal (40.4g fat, 38.6g protein, 1 g fiber)

These lamb chops are going to blow your mind with their incredible flavor! This flavorful meal has never failed to please anybody, and it has kept people coming back for more over the course of many years. It's appropriate for any event, including holidays like Thanksgiving and Christmas. Make preparations in advance, so that the lamb may sit in the marinade overnight.

Ingredients (5 servings)
15 (3 oz.) lamb loin chops (1-inch thick)
2 cloves garlic, sliced
1 teaspoon garlic powder, or to taste
1 pinch chili powder
2 tablespoons white sugar
Freshly ground black pepper, to taste
1 tablespoon fresh lime juice
1 tablespoon soy sauce
2 tablespoons olive oil
¼ cup chopped fresh cilantro
2 lime wedges
2 lemon wedges

Preparation

After placing the lamb chops in a roasting pan, season them with the minced garlic, garlic powder, chili powder, sugar, salt, and pepper until equally coated. Mix 1 tablespoon each of lime juice, soy sauce, and olive oil, and drizzle over the fish. Cover and refrigerate overnight. Turn the temperature in the oven up to 400 degrees F. (200 degrees C). While the oven is being preheated, the lamb should be allowed to come to room temperature.

Roast in an oven that has been warmed at the right temperature, about 20 minutes for medium or 30 minutes for well done, depending on how done you want the meat. Before serving, garnish each portion with a sprinkling of chopped cilantro and a generous amount of freshly squeezed lemon and lime juice.

Vietnamese Beef and Lettuce Curry

Preparation time: 15 minutes
Cook time: 45 minutes
Nutrition facts (per serving): 529 Cal (21g fat, 26.3g protein, 0.6 g fiber)

A wonderful and easy-to-make curry that may be served over steamed or boiling rice. Yet it's on the milder side of the curry spectrum. For Western palates who are used to eating lettuce exclusively in salads and buffet foods, the use of lettuce in cooked dishes is an exciting and unique departure from the norm.

Ingredients (4 servings)
1 cup uncooked long grain white rice
2 cups water
5 teaspoons white sugar
1 clove garlic, minced
¼ cup fish sauce
5 tablespoons water
1 ½ tablespoons chili sauce
1 lemon, juiced
2 tablespoons vegetable oil
3 cloves garlic, minced
1 lb. ground beef
1 tablespoon ground cumin
1 (28 oz.) can canned diced tomatoes
2 cups lettuce leaves, torn into ½-inch-wide strips

Preparation

Rice and water should be brought to a boil in a separate container. Turn the heat down to low, cover, and let it simmer for 25 minutes. Utilizing a pestle, combine the sugar and one garlic clove that has been peeled in a bowl. Combine the fish sauce, water, chili sauce, and lemon juice before mixing them all together. 3 cloves of garlic should be swiftly sautéed in the oil that has been heated in a wok over high heat.

The beef should be mixed in the wok, seasoned with cumin, and cooked until brown all over. The tomatoes and almost half of the fish sauce combination should be poured into the pan. Turn the heat down to low and let the mixture simmer for 20 minutes, or until it has thickened. Combine the lettuce with the ground beef in a bowl. As soon as it is ready, serve immediately over the cooked rice with the leftover fish sauce mixture on the side.

Vietnamese Beef and Red Cabbage Bowl

Preparation time: 25 minutes

Cook time: 5 minutes

Nutrition facts (per serving): 410 Cal (g fat, 23.8g protein, 6.1 g fiber)

I like the robust flavors that are typical of Vietnamese cuisine. This is quite stunning to look at, not to mention it's loaded with taste and spice. I've made the dish in individual bowls before, but I find that eating it family-style is more enjoyable. To add even more delicious magnificence to the dish, serve with spring rolls and jasmine rice of good quality. If you like things on the spicy side, try slicing up some habanero peppers and adding them to the dish.

Ingredients (4 servings)

1 head red cabbage

1 red onion, halved

3 tablespoons canola oil, divided

1 lb. lean ground beef

1 red Fresno chili pepper, sliced very thinly

2 teaspoons paprika

1 teaspoon kosher salt

2 tablespoons lime juice

1 tablespoon fish sauce

1 teaspoon packed brown sugar

½ teaspoon grated lime zest

½ cup chopped fresh cilantro

¼ cup chopped fresh mint

1 lime, cut into wedges

Preparation

On a horizontal surface, half the cabbage head lengthwise. To make a bowl, remove one half of the core and the majority of the leaves from the inside of the plant. The other half should be sliced very thinly. Half of the red onion should be chopped very finely, while the other half should be sliced very thinly. In a large pan, bring 1 tablespoon of canola oil up to temperature over medium heat. Mix in the ground meat, diced onion, Fresno chili pepper, paprika, and salt. Cook the meat for 5 to 7 minutes, breaking it up and turning it regularly, until it has browned and become crumbly. In a small bowl, combine the remaining oil, lime juice, fish sauce, brown sugar, and lime zest. Whisk until well combined. Combine everything by stirring it together in the meat mixture. Transfer the hot mixture to the basin made of cabbage. Add the sliced cabbage, sliced onion, cilantro, and mint to the top of the dish. Serve with slices of fresh lime.

Vietnamese BLT Wraps

Preparation time: 10 minutes
Nutrition facts (per serving): 132 Cal (12g fat, 2g protein, 2g fiber)

This gluten-free take on the classic BLT sandwich has a flavor punch that's inspired by Vietnamese cuisine. This recipe only produces four wraps, but it's very easy to double the ingredients to feed a large group.

Ingredients (4 servings)
4 bacon slices, cooked until crisp
4 large Bibb lettuce leaves
4 tablespoons Avocado Aioli (see associated recipes)
4 cilantro sprigs
4 mint sprigs
4 Thai basil sprigs
4 tablespoons Pickled Carrots and Daikon (see associated recipes)
1 heirloom tomato, cored and cut into wedges
2 tablespoons sliced Pickled Peppers (see associated recipes)

Preparation
Place a piece of bacon in the center of each leaf of lettuce. After drizzling with the aioli, top with the herbs, tomato wedges, carrot and daikon pickles, and pickled peppers in the order listed. Wrap it up, and have fun!

Vietnamese Caramelized Pork

Preparation time: 15 minutes

Cook time: 20 minutes

Nutrition facts (per serving): 657 Cal (34.7g fat, 29.9g protein, 1.2g fiber)

Tet Nguyen Dan, also known as the Vietnamese New Year, is the most significant event in Vietnam. On this occasion, people traditionally eat a meal called thit kho to, which consists of sticky-sweet pork with funkier overtones from nuoc mam. This dish is an adaptation of a recipe that was created by Michael Bao Huynh, a chef and restaurant who arrived in the United States as a refugee in 1982.

Ingredients (servings)

1 ½ cups sugar

2 ½ lbs. pork belly or butt, sliced into thin, inch-long strips

1 tablespoon salt

½ teaspoon freshly ground black pepper

¼ cup fish sauce

2 heaping teaspoons minced garlic

1 dash sesame oil

1 medium Vidalia onion, sliced

4 scallions, sliced, green part only

Rice, for serving

Preparation

Put 1 cup of sugar in the bottom of a big, heavy pan, and then set it over medium-low heat. After it has melted and become yellow, immediately add the pork, increase the heat to medium, and mix it until coated (The sugar may get sticky and may even become more solid as it cooks, but it will eventually remelt into a sauce.). Mix in the sugar, salt, pepper, and fish sauce left in the bowl. Cook for another minute with the cover on. Remove the cover, add the oil and garlic, and return to a boil for about 20 minutes to reduce the sauce.

After stirring in the Vidalia onions, continue cooking for 5 to 7 minutes, or until the onions become translucent. The pork should have a caramelized appearance; if it doesn't, increase the heat and sauté it while the sauce continues to decrease. Place in a serving basin and top with scallion greens before serving.

Vietnamese Crispy Fish

Preparation time: 15 minutes

Cook time: 16 minutes

Nutrition facts (per serving): 401 Cal (17g fat, 48.3 protein, 0.4g fiber)

Snapper is a fish that stands up exceptionally well to this cooking because of its sweet and spicy flavor, but you may use any fish that you choose. You could also use fillets instead of the entire fish, but if you really want to wow people, the whole fish is the way to go. Rice should be served with it.

Ingredients (4 servings)

1.5 lbs. whole fish

½ teaspoon salt

¼ teaspoon ground black pepper

½ teaspoon ground turmeric

⅓ cup chopped lemongrass

3 garlic cloves (minced)

½ teaspoon red pepper flakes (optional)

¼ cup vegetable oil

¼ cup corn starch

Preparation

After giving it a thorough cleaning, pat the fish dry with paper towels. On both sides of the fish, cut a few diagonal slashes into the flesh. Salt, pepper, turmeric, lemongrass, garlic, and red pepper flakes should be combined in a small bowl and mixed together (optional). Apply a generous amount of the mixture all over the fish, being sure to get it in between the slits and within the hollow. Corn starch should be used to coat the fish in a very thin coating.

Warm the vegetable oil on a medium-low heat in a skillet that is non-stick and has a cover. After adding the fish, cover the pan with the lid to keep it warm. Fry for approximately 5 minutes while keeping the heat low and covered. The cover will help keep in the heat, which will assist in cooking the fish all the way through. Keep an eye out for splatters of oil. The garlic and lemongrass won't catch fire if the heat is kept at a low simmer. Although it's true that the fish won't become crispy if the lid is on the pan, we'll still get it nice and browned in the end.

After turning the fish over, continue cooking it on the lowest heat setting with the lid on for another 5 minutes. Now take the top off the pot, and while keeping the heat at medium-high, crank it up just a little. The intense heat will cause the skin to become crisp. Cook for 1 to 2 minutes. Fry until crispy on the opposite side for one to two minutes after you flip it. Move the fish to a dish that has been lined with paper towels in order to absorb any extra oil. Serve with steamed rice, sliced cucumbers, tomatoes, fresh greens, and a fish sauce dipping sauce on the side, if desired.

Vietnamese Eggplant with Spicy Sauce

Preparation time: 25 minutes

Cook time: 11 minutes

Nutrition facts (per serving): 273 Cal (21.2g fat, 3.3g protein, 9.5g fiber)

This dish is one that I learned to make in a cooking school in Hoi An, Vietnam. This eggplant preparation method is both tasty and straightforward. Now this is a recipe that everyone in the family loves! Garnish with chopped green onion and fresh basil before serving.

Ingredients (2 servings)

3 tablespoons vegetable oil, divided

1 white eggplant, sliced

3 tablespoons minced lemongrass

1 tablespoon crushed garlic

1 tablespoon chopped green onion

1 tablespoon chopped fresh basil

1 teaspoon minced red chili pepper

1 teaspoon minced fresh ginger

1 tablespoon oyster sauce

1 teaspoon white sugar

Preparation

In a pan, bring one tablespoon of oil up to temperature over medium heat. After adding the eggplant, sauté it for three to five minutes each side, or until golden brown and tender, but not mushy. In a dish, combine the remaining 2 tablespoons of oil, the second half of the lemongrass, the garlic, the green onion, the basil, and the red chili. Pour over eggplant in the skillet. About three minutes into the cooking process, the green onion should be wilted. Add the oyster sauce and sugar and stir to combine. Cook for 2 to 3 minutes, or until the flavors have combined. Take the pan off the heat.

Vietnamese Fresh Spring Rolls

Preparation time: 45 minutes

Cook time: 5 minutes

Nutrition facts (per serving): 82 Cal (0.7g fat, 3.3 g protein, 0.6 g fiber)

These baked spring rolls are a welcome departure from the traditional fried kind and have quickly become a fan favorite in the home. They're so fantastic as a light appetizer to serve during the warm summer months, and they taste wonderful when dipped in either of the sauces.

Ingredients (8 servings)

2 oz. rice vermicelli

8 rice wrappers (8.5-inch diameter)

8 large cooked shrimp - peeled, deveined, and cut in half

1⅓ tablespoons chopped fresh Thai basil

3 tablespoons chopped fresh mint leaves

3 tablespoons chopped fresh cilantro

2 leaves lettuce, chopped

4 teaspoons fish sauce

¼ cup water

2 tablespoons fresh lime juice

1 clove garlic, minced

2 tablespoons white sugar

½ teaspoon garlic chili sauce

3 tablespoons hoisin sauce

1 teaspoon finely chopped peanuts

Preparation

Start the boiling process with some water in a pot of medium size. Boil rice vermicelli 3 to 5 minutes, or until al dente, then drain. Warm water should be added to a big dish. To soften one of the wrappers, dunk it into the hot water for one second. Place the wrapper on its side. Place 2 shrimp halves, a handful of vermicelli, basil, mint, and cilantro, and some lettuce in a row in the middle of the platter, making sure to leave approximately 2 inches of space on each side.

After folding the exposed edges inside, coil the wrapper securely, starting at the end with the lettuce. Proceed in the same manner with the remaining ingredients. Combine the fish sauce, water, lime juice, garlic, sugar, and chili sauce in a small bowl and stir to combine. Combine the hoisin sauce and peanuts in a separate, similarly sized bowl. The fish sauce and hoisin sauce combinations should be served with the wrapped spring rolls.

Vietnamese Golden Chicken Wings

Preparation time: 15 minutes

Cook time: 30 minutes

Nutrition facts (per serving): 716 Cal (50.9g fat, 53g protein, 0.8g fiber)

This delicious Vietnamese cuisine is perfect for any occasion, from weekday dinners to parties and barbecues, or even just a night spent in front of the television! The chicken wings have a juicy flavor, and the flesh is so tender and flavorful that it almost melts in your mouth. They have a crunchy outside, but the inside is nice and chewy, and they're certain to be a hit. They have never failed to leave an impression on me!

Ingredients (4 servings)

¼ cup Asian fish sauce

2 tablespoons fresh lemon juice

2 tablespoons sesame oil

1 teaspoon salt

1 teaspoon freshly ground black pepper

1 tablespoon garlic powder

1 tablespoon white sugar

Preparation

Put the chicken wings, garlic cloves, and onion slices into a large bowl. Pour in soy sauce, fish sauce, lemon juice, and sesame oil. Add some salt, pepper, garlic powder, and sugar, then mix everything together so that everything is evenly covered. Cover and place in the refrigerator for at least 2 hours and up to overnight. Set the temperature in the oven to 400 degrees F. (200 degrees C). Prepare a baking dish measuring 9x13 inches by lining it with aluminum foil.

Take the wings out of the marinade, but being sure to set some aside. Place the wings in a single layer over the bottom of the dish that has been prepared. Bake in an oven that has been warmed, flipping once and coating with the remaining marinade, for about 30 minutes, or until the meat is deep golden brown and the juices flow clear.

Vietnamese Grilled Lemongrass Chicken

Preparation time: 10 minutes
Cook time: 10 minutes
Nutrition facts (per serving): 308 Cal (19g fat, 29g protein, 0.1 g fiber)

Grilled chicken that has been seasoned with lemongrass marinade. Rice paper, lettuce, cucumber, bean sprouts, mint, and ground peanut should be used as garnishes for this dish.

Ingredients (4 servings)

2 tablespoons canola oil

2 tablespoons finely chopped lemongrass

1 tablespoon lemon juice

2 teaspoons soy sauce

2 teaspoons light brown sugar

2 teaspoons minced garlic

1 teaspoon fish sauce

1½ lbs. chicken thighs, or more to taste, pounded to an even thickness

Preparation

In a large mixing bowl, combine the canola oil, lemongrass, lemon juice, soy sauce, brown sugar, garlic, and fish sauce until the sugar is dissolved. Add the chicken and flip it to coat it in the marinade. Marinate the chicken in the refrigerator for up to an hour, starting 20 minutes before serving. Prepare the grill with a heat setting of medium and grease the grate gently. Take the chicken thighs out of the marinade and give them a good shake to get rid of any excess. Throw away the marinade that is left over. Cook the chicken on the grill for 3 to 5 minutes each side, or until the center is no longer pink and the juices run clear. If you place an instant-read thermometer into the middle, it should register at least 165 degrees Fahrenheit (74 degrees C).

Vietnamese Grilled Pork Skewers

Preparation time: 30 minutes

Cook time: 8 minutes

Nutrition facts (per serving): 204 Cal (10.6g fat, 10.8g protein, 0.3 g fiber)

We need to have two items ready in order to make this cuisine: the pig that has been barbecued, and the sauce for dipping it.

Ingredients (servings)

1 lb. pork belly, cubed

1 fresh red chili pepper, minced

3 stalks lemongrass, minced

3 tablespoons fish sauce

3 cloves garlic, minced, or more to taste

1 teaspoon monosodium glutamate (MSG)

1 teaspoon white sugar

1 teaspoon Chinese five-spice powder

Dipping Sauce

¼ cup fish sauce

¼ cup white sugar

1 fresh red chili pepper, minced, or more to taste

1 lime, juiced

5 cloves garlic, minced, or more to taste

1 teaspoon monosodium glutamate (MSG), or to taste

1 cup water

Preparation

In a bowl, combine the pork belly, 1 red chili pepper, lemongrass, 3 cloves of garlic, 3 tablespoons of fish sauce, 1 teaspoon of MSG, 1 teaspoon of white sugar, and five-spice powder. Cover with plastic wrap and place in the refrigerator for between 1 and 3 hours to let the marinade to absorb. In a bowl, combine ¼ of a cup of fish sauce, ¼ of a cup of sugar, one red chili pepper, lime juice, 5 cloves of garlic, and 1 teaspoon of MSG. Allow it rest for up to an hour so that the flavors of the dipping sauce may combine. Pour in the water. Wrap the pork belly in the marinade and then thread it onto bamboo skewers. Prepare the grill for high heat and oil the grate just a little bit. Cook the pork skewers over medium-high heat, flipping them regularly, for 8 to 10 minutes. Serve with the accompanying dipping sauce.

Vietnamese Lemon Grass Chicken Curry

Preparation time: 15 minutes
Cook time: 25 minutes
Nutrition facts (per serving): 813 Cal (58.4g fat, 63.8g protein, 0.3g fiber)

This recipe for fragrant, mildly spicy chicken curry was handed down to me from my Vietnamese grandmother and creates the very greatest chicken curry there has ever been. The key is to use freshly chopped lemongrass! When served over white or sticky rice, you'll feel like you've died and gone to paradise.

Ingredients (servings)
2 tablespoons vegetable oil
1 lemongrass, minced
1 (3 lb.) whole chicken, cut into pieces
⅔ cup water
1 tablespoon fish sauce
1½ tablespoons curry powder
1 tablespoon cornstarch
1 tablespoon chopped cilantro, optional

Preparation
Heat the vegetable oil in a pan over medium heat. After stirring in the lemongrass, continue to simmer for another three to five minutes until the aroma is released. Put the chicken in the pan and start cooking it.

After approximately ten minutes of cooking with stirring, the chicken is done when no longer pink in the middle and the skin has become brown.

Mix the fish sauce, curry powder, and water together in a bowl. Raise the temperature to high, and bring the liquid to a boil. Turn the heat down to a simmer and cook for 10 to 15 minutes. In a small bowl, whisk together cornstarch and 2 tablespoons of the curry sauce until the mixture is smooth. The cornstarch mixture should be stirred into the pan and then the sauce should be left to boil for approximately 5 minutes until it has thickened. Before serving, sprinkle the dish with cilantro.

Appetizers and Salad

Spicy Vietnamese Quick Pickled Vegetables

Preparation time: 20 minutes
Cook time: 10 minutes
Nutrition facts (per serving): 27 Cal (0.1g fat,0.7 g protein, 1.3g fiber)

These quickly pickled veggies are generally used as a condiment for banh mi sandwiches. However, they also make a delicious side dish for anything that you would ordinarily pair with coleslaw, such as fish and chips, barbecue, fish tacos, and so on.

Ingredients (10 servings)

½ lb. carrots, peeled and cut into matchsticks
½ lb. purple daikon radish, peeled and cut into matchsticks
½ lb. English cucumber, sliced into thin rounds
2 jalapeno peppers, sliced into rings
2 cups water
1 ½ cups rice vinegar
2 tablespoons white sugar
2 teaspoons salt

Preparation

Examine 2 canning jars for any signs of damage, such as cracks or rust on the lids or rings, and dispose of any that are flawed. Keep veggies submerged in water that is simmering until they are ready to eat. Rings and lids that are brand new should be washed in warm soapy water before use. Carrots, radishes, cucumbers, and jalapeño peppers should each have an equal amount of space in one of the 2 clean jars.

In a medium-sized saucepan, mix together the water, vinegar, sugar, and salt. Bring to a boil and continue cooking for approximately 3 minutes, or until the sugar has dissolved. Remove the pan from the heat and wait 2 minutes for it to cool down. After pouring the liquid over the veggies that are contained in the jars, let it to reach room temperature for approximately half an hour. Replace the lids and place the containers in the refrigerator for at least an hour before serving.

Garnish Plate for Pho

Preparation time: 5 minute
Cook time: 5 minutes
Nutrition facts (per serving): 176 Cal (3.9g fat, 17.3g protein, 0.9 g fiber)

Lime juice may be harsh and overpower the other tastes in pho. During the spring and summer, when the weather is warmer, I like to use Thai basil (hung qu), which is at its height, as well as a sort of spicy mint (hung cay) that is offered in Vietnamese markets. When I have an appetite for bean sprouts, I'll go out and get ones that are really fresh, and then I'll blanch them to reduce the intensity of their taste and smooth out their texture.

Ingredients (servings)

2 handfuls bean sprouts
2 or 3 sprigs mint, regular or spicy
2 or 3 sprigs Thai basil
3 or 4 fresh culantro leaves
2 or 3 sprigs rice paddy herb
1 lime, cut into wedges
1 Thai chili or ½ jalapeño, Fresno, or serrano chili, thinly sliced

Preparation

If you want to blanch the bean sprouts, you should include this step into the process of assembling the pho and utilize the pot that has been prepared for immersing the noodles; the strainer for the noodles is ideal for this task. They should be blanched before you start working on the noodles to prevent the starch from coating them, and you should arrange them on a separate dish so that they don't drip water on the other garnishes.

In any other case, place the raw sprouts, herbs, and lime on a large communal platter. If the chili is on the smaller side, cut it at an acute angle to produce pieces that are quite large and can be distinguished from one another in the bowl. Place the slices in a small plate to prevent them from being misplaced. Set the garnishes and any additional sides or condiments on the table before you assemble the bowls, so that you can start eating as soon as the bowls are ready.

Ginger Dipping Sauce

Preparation time: 5 minutes

Cook time: 20 minutes

Nutrition facts (per serving): 119 Cal (0g fat, 2 g protein, 1g fiber)

A lot of folks like their chicken pho accompanied by a side of this fiery sauce. They do this while eating soup by dipping the meat into the sauce. Some people find the fresh ginger taste to be an exhilarating and exciting addition to the flavor profile, while others find it to be distracting and unnecessary. Put it to the test, and decide for yourself.

Ingredients (servings)

2 tablespoons peeled and finely chopped ginger

6 tablespoons fresh lime juice

2 ½ tablespoons sugar

3 tablespoons fish sauce

2 teaspoons finely chopped seeded Fresno or jalapeño chili pepper

Preparation

Ginger, lime juice, and sugar should be mixed together in a small bowl and then stirred to dissolve the sugar. Try it out to see whether the balance of spiciness, acidity, and sweetness is to your liking. Adjust as required. After adding the fish sauce and the chili, leave the bowl aside for 15 minutes to allow the flavors to combine and develop. It's possible to store the sauce in the refrigerator for a few days. Serve directly from the bowl, or use it as a dressing for a salad.

Cha Gio Vietnamese Egg Rolls

Preparation time: 45 minutes

Cook time: 5 minutes

Nutrition facts (per serving): 227 Cal (13.5g fat, 12 g protein, 0 g fiber)

They can be stored for a long time in the freezer, you should definitely prepare a second batch of these egg rolls. For a unique spin on this dish, try adding shredded cabbage or julienned taro. You may boost the taste by adding crab meat in minced form.

Ingredients (12 servings)

1 cup uncooked bean threads (cellophane noodles)

1 large dried shiitake mushroom

1 lb. ground pork

½ lb. shrimp, chopped

1 large carrot, peeled and grated

1 small shallot, minced

2 ¼ teaspoons Vietnamese fish sauce

1 ¼ teaspoon white sugar

1 ¼ teaspoons salt

1 ¼ teaspoon ground black pepper

24 egg roll wrappers

1 egg, beaten

Oil, for deep frying

Preparation

Vermicelli and shiitake mushrooms should be soaked in warm water until flexible, which should take around 15 minutes; then they should be drained well. Shiitake should be minced. Vermicelli, shiitake mushrooms, pork, shrimp, carrots, shallots, fish sauce, sugar, salt, and pepper should all be mixed together in a big dish. To ensure that the filling components are distributed equally and that the pork is broken up, toss the mixture well. Place 1 egg roll wrapper on a flat surface in a diagonal position.

A little less than 2 teaspoons of filling should be spread over the middle of the wrapper. To surround the filling, fold the bottom corner over the filling, and then fold in the side corners. Egg should be brushed on the top corner of the wrapper, then rolling should be continued to seal it. Make other egg rolls in a similar way. The oil should be heated to 350 degrees Fahrenheit (175 degrees Celsius) in a deep-fryer, wok, or big saucepan or until a drop of water will jump on the top. Fry egg rolls until they are golden brown, which should take between 5 and 8 minutes. Paper towels or paper bags may be used for draining.

Crispy Fried Shallots

Preparation time: 10 minutes
Cook time: 30 minutes
Nutrition facts (per serving): 25 Cal (1 g fat, 0 g protein, 0 g fiber)

Shallots that have been cooked till they are golden and crisp are a traditional condiment in Vietnam. They may be found in soups and on salads, used as a garnish for dumplings, and chopped up and used to meatballs. They're essential because of their crunchiness, sweetness, and saltiness. Because it is so difficult for folks to resist the temptation to munch on them, you may want to consider doubling the recipe. After you have finished frying the shallots, strain the oil and save it to use in other dishes or to cook more shallots. The strained oil, also known as shallot oil, has a shelf life of several weeks when stored in the refrigerator. It's best to utilize the fried shallots on the same day that you prepare them.

Ingredients (2 servings)
2 cups thinly sliced shallots (about 4 large shallots)
2 cups canola oil

Preparation
Place a medium heatproof bowl over a fine-mesh sieve. Mandolin-slice shallots into rings, crosswise. Pour enough oil into a medium saucepan to completely cover the shallots. For 20–25 minutes, sauté the shallots, turning often with a fork to help them split into rings. Drain the shallots by putting them in a colander and then onto paper towels. Allow to cool

after seasoning with salt. If you're going to use shallot oil, save it for other things like vinaigrettes, stir-fries, or soups. It's even possible to fry the shallots a week in advance. At room temperature, keep it sealed tightly.

Nuoc Cham

Preparation time: 5 minutes
Cook time: 5 minutes
Nutrition facts (per serving): 29 Cal (0g fat, 0 g protein, 0g fiber)

Nuoc Cham is essentially a combination of water, sugar, lime juice, and fish sauce; this combination forms the foundation of the taste profile that's characteristic of Vietnamese cuisine. This is an excellent sauce that can bring out the flavor of seafood, add a salty tang to beef or pork, or soak into a bowl of vermicelli for a delicious snack.

Ingredients (16 servings)
1 cup hot water
½ cup white sugar
½ cup freshly squeezed lime juice
⅓ cup Vietnamese fish sauce
2 medium cloves garlic, minced
1 small bird's eye chili, minced optional

Preparation
Whisk the water and sugar together in a small bowl until the sugar is completely dissolved. Mix all of the ingredients well after adding the lime juice, fish sauce, garlic, and chili, if using. Either use it right away or keep it in a jar that seals tightly in the refrigerator.

Nuoc Cham Vietnamese Dipping Sauce

Preparation time: 15 minutes
Nutrition facts (per serving): 15 Cal (0g fat, 0.4g protein, 0g fiber)

Try my own touch on a tried-and-true dipping sauce. A touch of sweetness, but the predominant flavor is savory, and there is a pleasant amount of heat. To allow the flavors to meld, I prepare this at least 24 hours in advance of when I want to use it. When stored in an airtight container in the refrigerator, sauce that has been used before may be preserved for up to 4 weeks. Experiment with other things what's expressed here doesn't appeal to you.

Ingredients (20 servings)
¼ cup white sugar
½ cup warm water
¼ cup fish sauce
⅓ cup distilled white vinegar
½ lemon, juiced
3 cloves garlic, minced
3 Thai chili peppers, chopped
1 green onion, thinly slice

Preparation
Put the carrots in a separate bowl. Add the other ingredients into a small bowl and whisk them together until the sugar is fully dissolved. Just before serving, include the carrots into the dish. If you want things on the hotter side, you may also use chili garlic sauce.

Duck Bamboo Salad

Preparation time: 30 minutes

Cook time: 30 minutes

Nutrition facts (per serving): 265 Cal (25.5g fat, 15.9g protein, 0.2g fiber)

The fresh aroma of spring: European duck with an olive twist and a bamboo salad made in the Vietnamese style. One of the most flavorful cuts of red meat is duck. The combination of the duck from Europe and the fresh bamboo from Vietnam results in a flavor that's all its own.

Ingredients (2 servings)

1 duck breast

⅓ oz. sliced olives

⅓ oz. dried apricots

1 oz. butter

2 oz. baby arugula

1 teaspoon salt

Pepper, to taste

11 oz. fresh bamboo (canned is ok)

2 oz. roasted peanuts

Dressing

1 chili pepper

1 oz. sugar

2 tablespoons fish sauce

2 tablespoons lemon juice

2 teaspoons chopped shallot

2 teaspoons chopped garlic

1 teaspoon chopped ginger

Preparation

Prepare a marinade for the duck breast by seasoning it with salt and pepper. Put the pan on the burner, then turn the duck breasts so that the skin side is facing down, and gradually raise the temperature so that the duck may produce more fat. After frying for about 4 minutes to get a browned appearance on both sides, the duck breast should be transferred to a platter. Wait for a break of 5 minutes before starting the second round of frying.

While the duck breast is resting, prepare the fresh bamboo shoots by placing them in a saucepan, giving them a quick boil for 5 minutes, and then rinsing them in cold water. The bamboo shoots should be placed in a bowl, and the olives, apricots, and shallots should be added to the dish. In order to prepare the dressing, combine water, sugar, and lemon juice in a dish and stir with chopsticks until the sugar is completely dissolved. Mix in some fish sauce, chopped chili, garlic, shallot, and ginger.

Prepare the duck breast by heating a skillet on the stovetop and frying it until it is done. To ensure that the duck breast is cooked through evenly, add 1 oz. of butter and pour the melted butter over it (about 4 minutes is enough). Check to see that the duck is cooked thoroughly but is still little pink in the middle. It shouldn't be overcooked or it will be dry. Before slicing the duck breast, give it a rest for 4 minutes first.

To prepare the dish, combine the bamboo with the dressing. On a dish, arrange the bamboo shoots, then slice the duck breast and arrange it on top of the slices. Add some chopped peanuts and baby Rocca on top.

Cucumber Tomato and Pineapple Salad with Asian Dressing

Preparation time: 30 minutes
Cook time: 30 minutes
Nutrition facts (per serving): 79 Cal (5g fat, 1g protein,1 g fiber)

This genuinely spectacular salad with a Vietnamese influence is the essence of taste synergy, as it combines savory ingredients like serrano peppers and sweet pineapple with refreshing herbs like cucumber and mint.

Ingredients (6 servings)
1 large garlic clove
¼ teaspoon salt
2 tablespoons fresh lime juice
1 tablespoon sugar
2 tablespoons vegetable oil
1 (2-inch-long) fresh serrano or jalapeño chili pepper, minced, including seeds
¼ to ½ teaspoon Asian fish sauce
½ seedless cucumber (often plastic-wrapped), halved lengthwise, then thinly sliced crosswise
½ pineapple, peeled, quartered lengthwise, cored, then sliced crosswise ¼ inch thick
½ cup coarsely chopped fresh cilantro
¼ cup coarsely chopped fresh mint
2 medium tomatoes, cut into ½-inch-thick wedges

Preparation

First, mince the garlic, and then using the side of a big heavy knife, crush it into a paste with the salt. Lime juice and sugar should be whisked together in a big bowl until the sugar is dissolved, after which the oil, garlic paste, chili, and fish sauce should be whisked in (to taste). Salt should be added to taste after the other ingredients have been incorporated and tossed.

Asian Noodle Salad with Shrimp

Preparation time: 30 minutes
Cook time: 30 minutes
Nutrition facts (per serving): 89 Cal (2g fat, 4g protein, 1g fiber)

These chilled noodles prepared in the manner of Vietnamese cuisine are just what the doctor ordered for a hot night. You may get rice stick noodles, fish sauce, and chili-garlic sauce in the Asian department of many supermarkets as well as in Asian markets.

Ingredients (4 servings)

1 (6.75 oz.) package rice stick noodles (maifun)

4 ½ tablespoons fresh lime juice

3 tablespoons fish sauce (such as nam pla or nuoc nam)

4 teaspoons chili-garlic sauce

2 teaspoons sugar

1 lb. peeled deveined cooked medium shrimp

1 cup thinly sliced Japanese cucumbers or Persian cucumbers

1 (8 oz.) package sugar snap peas, cut crosswise into ½-inch pieces

1 red bell pepper, thinly sliced

½ cup (loosely packed) fresh mint leaves

½ cup (loosely packed) fresh cilantro leaves

Preparation

Prepare the items that are fresh. Put all of the ingredients for the dressing or marinade into a liquid measuring cup. Whisk until everything is well blended. Marinate the shrimp in a bowl containing half of the mixture by first pouring it into the bowl. Put the remaining portion in the refrigerator (this will be the dressing for the salad). Prepare the soba noodles for eating. After grilling the shrimp, combine them with the noodles and sauce in a large bowl.

Summer Steak Salad with Ginger and Lime Dressing

Preparation time: 10 minutes

Cook time: 5 minutes

Nutrition facts (per serving): 534 Cal (32g fat, 33g protein, 4 g fiber, 1584mg)

This traditional Vietnamese dish, which is popular across Asia and goes by the name bo luc lac, is produced by shaking the steak in a very hot skillet, which effectively gives it a seared texture. Rice flavored with jasmine or brown rice will go well with this dish.

Ingredients (4 servings)

3 tablespoons fish sauce

2 tablespoons sugar

2 tablespoons fresh lime juice

2 tablespoons water

1 tablespoon minced peeled fresh ginger

2 garlic cloves, minced

1 teaspoon minced red jalapeño chili pepper

Salad

2 tablespoons oyster sauce

1 tablespoon medium-dry Sherry

2 teaspoons tamari soy sauce

2 garlic cloves, minced

1 teaspoon (packed) brown sugar

1 ¼ lbs. New York steak, trimmed, cut into ⅔-inch cubes

2 bunches watercress, bottom 2 inches discarded, cut into 1-inch lengths

3 cups mizuna leaves, torn in half if very large

2 cups (lightly packed) torn Bibb lettuce leaves

1 cup Thai basil leaves, cut into ½-inch-wide strips

½ (12 oz.) English hothouse cucumber, halved lengthwise, sliced very thinly on diagonal

12 cherry tomatoes

2 tablespoons vegetable oil

½ medium-size red onion, cut into thin wedges

2 shallots, sliced into thin rounds

¼ medium pineapple, peeled, cored, halved lengthwise, cut crosswise into ⅓-inch-thick slices

Preparation

In a small bowl, whisk together all of the ingredients to combine them.

Salad

In a medium bowl, combine the following ingredients: oyster sauce, Sherry, tamari soy sauce, minced garlic, and brown sugar. Stir in steak. Marinate the steak for at least half an hour and up to 2 hours, turning it over every so often. A big bowl should be used to combine watercress, mizuna, lettuce, basil, cucumber, and tomatoes. Toss the mixture after adding half of the dressing. Prepare a big dish with a rim and arrange the greens combination on it.

Bring the oil to a high temperature in a big nonstick skillet. Sauté the onion and shallot for 30 seconds after adding them. Mix in the meat with the marinade. It should take around 4 minutes of sautéing until the meat is browned on the surface but is still pink within. After adding the pineapple slices, continue stirring them for about one more minute until they are completely warmed through. Place the steak combination along with any remaining liquids from the pan on top of the dressed greens mixture that is on the dish. Serve the salad topped with the remaining dressing drizzled over it.

Sweet Salty Beef Salad

Preparation time: 10 minutes
Cook time: 35 minutes
Nutrition facts (per serving): 336 Cal (12g fat, 30g protein, 4g fiber)

Here's a salad that exemplifies the yin and yang principle of blending tastes that are diametrically opposed to one another. Iceberg lettuce, which has a mild taste and a crisp texture, helps the diverse flavors of the warm dressing—hot, sweet, sour, and salty—stand out.

Ingredients (2 servings)

1 ½ tablespoons fish sauce, or reduced-sodium soy sauce
1 ½ tablespoons brown sugar
½ head iceberg lettuce, halved, cored and thinly sliced
2 teaspoons canola oil, divided
8 oz. sirloin steak, trimmed and thinly sliced
1 jalapeño, or serrano pepper, seeded and minced
1 small onion, finely chopped
1 clove garlic, minced
1 orange, peel and white pith removed, coarsely chopped
2 tablespoons chopped fresh cilantro
1 tablespoon chopped dry-roasted peanuts

Preparation

Brown sugar and fish sauce, or soy sauce, should be mixed together in a small basin. Divide lettuce between 2 plates. 1 teaspoon of oil should be heated in a medium nonstick skillet over medium-high heat until the oil shimmers but doesn't start to smoke. After adding the beef, continue to heat it while stirring for 1 to 2 minutes, or until it has browned on the exterior but is still pink on the inside. Place a spoonful on top of the lettuce.

After adding the remaining 1 teaspoon of oil, the jalapeño (or serrano), onion, and garlic to the pan, heat the mixture for approximately a minute while stirring until the aroma is released. After removing the pan from the heat, whisk in the orange and cilantro, then add the combination of fish sauce (or soy sauce). The salad should be topped with the peanuts and the sauce should be spooned over it.

Table Salad

Preparation time: 20 minutes
Cook time: 20 minutes
Nutrition facts (per serving): 359 Cal (4g fat,34 g protein, 10g fiber)

There are two primary applications for a table salad in Vietnam. Firstly, as an accompaniment to meals in which bite-sized portions of meat and fish are wrapped in the lettuce and eaten out of hand. Secondly, as a salad that may be used for a variety of purposes.

Ingredients (2 servings)

2 cups loosely packed spring mix
1 cup loosely packed baby arugula
2 seedless mini cucumbers, sliced into rounds
1 large red bell pepper, roasted (or you can use jarred roasted red peppers)
Red onion slices, to taste
Kalamata olives, to taste
4 oz. cubed chicken
Salt and pepper, to taste

Preparation

Put all of the components into a significant bowl. Then you should use the chopper to run all of the ingredients through it until they are chopped to the proper consistency. Alternately, you may use a chopping board to finely chop everything and then transfer it all to a big bowl before proceeding with the dressing. You may also turn this as a standard salad with toppings rather than a chopped salad if you want. After that, drizzle on some of your preferred dressing and stir it in.

Vietnamese Chicken Noodle Salad

Preparation time: 5 minutes

Cook time: 40 minutes

Nutrition facts (per serving): 402 Cal (12g fat, 32g protein, 4g fiber)

Fish sauce is the Southeast Asian equivalent of soy sauce; while it has a more assertive flavor at first taste, it becomes very fragrant and adaptable when mixed with other ingredients, such as the chicken, veggies, and peanuts in this zesty, revitalizing salad.

Ingredients (servings)

4 oz. rice noodles

½ cucumber

5 oz. leftover cooked chicken, shredded

1 medium carrot, cut into thin matchsticks

3 sprigs mint, leaves chopped, plus a few more for garnish

large handful beansprouts

2 oz. salted peanuts, roughly chopped, to serve

Dressing

½ lime, zested and juiced

2 tablespoon soft brown sugar

2 tablespoon rice vinegar

2 tablespoon fish sauce

1 long red chili, deseeded, finely chopped (plus sliced extra thin for garnish)

Preparation

After cooking the noodles in accordance with the directions on the package, rinse them in cold water and transfer them to a big bowl. Cut the cucumber in half lengthwise, use a teaspoon to scoop out the seeds, and then use a peeler to cut the cucumber into thin ribbons. The beansprouts should be blanched for at least 15 seconds in water that is boiling, and then they should be allowed to cool.

Mix in the chicken, carrot, mint, and beansprouts after adding the ribbons to the noodles and before adding the chicken. First, combine all of the ingredients for the dressing in a separate bowl, and then pour it over the salad and toss it. When ready to serve, transfer the mixture to a serving tray and sprinkle with more peanuts, mint, and chili.

Vietnamese Chicken Cabbage Salad

Preparation time: 15 minutes
Cook time: 15 minutes
Nutrition facts (per serving): 206 Cal (8g fat, 21g protein, 3g fiber)

This simple Vietnamese salad is perfect for a warm evening in the summer. The aromas of onion, lemon, and salt are balanced out by the flavors of cabbage and chicken in this dish.

Ingredients (4 servings)

2 cups cooked and shredded chicken breasts
2 ½ cups shredded green cabbage
3 scallions, sliced
2 medium carrots, grated
3 tablespoons freshly squeezed lime juice
2 tablespoons fish sauce
1 tablespoon white sugar
1 tablespoon rice wine vinegar
3 tablespoons roughly chopped salted peanuts
¼ cup roughly chopped mint leaves

Preparation

Place the chicken, cabbage, onions, and carrots in a large bowl and toss them all together. Lime juice, fish sauce, sugar, and vinegar should all be combined in a small bowl and whisked together until the sugar is completely dissolved. After pouring the dressing over the salad, give it a good toss to evenly distribute it. Mix in the peanuts as well as the mint.

You may serve the dish at room temperature or with a mild cold temperature.

Vietnamese Chicken Salad

Preparation time: 30 minutes
Cook time: 15 minutes
Nutrition facts (per serving): 303 Cal (17.9g fat, 19.2g protein, 3g fiber)

Ingredients (4 servings)
3 chicken breast fillets
½ large wombok (Chinese cabbage), finely shredded
2 carrots, peeled, cut into matchsticks
1 cup fresh mint leaves
1 cup fresh coriander leaves
½ cup roasted salted peanuts, chopped

Vietnamese Dressing
⅓ cup lime juice
⅓ cup fish sauce
4 small red chilies, deseeded, finely chopped
2 tablespoon brown sugar

Preparation
Make the dressing by combining all ingredients for it. The chicken should be placed in a big pot. Fill the covering with ice water. Over medium heat, bring the liquid to a boil. Turn the heat down to low. Cover. Simmer for 10 to 12 minutes, flipping the meat once, or until it is completely cooked through. Take away from the heat. Cool. Shred. Chicken, cabbage, carrots, mint, and cilantro should all be combined in

a big dish. Dressing should be drizzled on top. Mix well by tossing. Add the chopped peanuts for garnish. Serve.

Vietnamese Mango Chicken Pizz'Alad

Preparation time: 10 minutes
Cook time: 1 hour
Nutrition facts (per serving): 366 Cal (8g fat, 18g protein, 6g fiber)

In this dish for sweet and spicy salad pizza, a crisp pizza crust is topped with a salad consisting of crispy cabbage, mango, and chicken that has been tossed in a dressing that is inspired by Vietnamese cuisine and is created with fish sauce and lime juice. To prevent the crust from getting soggy, you should be sure on serve the pizza as soon as you put the salad to the top of it. Bread flour provides the pizza crust a crisp and robust structure, although all-purpose flour may be used effectively in its stead if bread flour isn't available.

Ingredients (5 servings)
⅔ cup lukewarm water
1 teaspoon instant or rapid rise yeast
1 teaspoon sugar
1¼ cups bread flour or all-purpose flour
¾ cup white whole-wheat flour or all-purpose flour
½ teaspoon salt
3 tablespoons lime juice
2 tablespoons canola oil, divided
1 tablespoon light brown sugar
1 tablespoon fish sauce
1 tablespoon minced garlic
1 cup shredded cooked chicken
2 cups thinly sliced napa cabbage

2 cups thinly sliced red cabbage

½ cup grated carrot

¼ cup chopped fresh mint

2 scallions, sliced

1 fresh serrano or jalapeño pepper, minced

1 mango, chopped

Preparation

To make pizza dough: In a large bowl, combine the water, yeast, and sugar. Let the mixture rest for approximately 5 minutes, or until the yeast has dissolved. As the dough starts to come together, stir in the bread flour (or all-purpose flour), whole-wheat flour (or all-purpose flour), and salt. Turn the dough out onto a work surface that has been gently dusted with flour. Knead for approximately 10 minutes, or until the dough is smooth and elastic.

(Another option is to use a food processor to combine the ingredients for the dough. Process it until it comes together in a ball, then continue processing it for another minute to knead it.) Put the dough in a basin that has been greased, and flip it to coat it. When the dough has about doubled in size, after approximately an hour of resting in a warm location that's free of drafts, cover the bowl with a clean kitchen towel and leave it away.

Lime juice, brown sugar, fish sauce, and garlic should be mixed together in a big bowl. Add 1 tablespoon of oil. After adding the chicken, give everything a good swirl to coat it, then leave it aside to marinade while you make the pizza. Place a pizza stone on the rack that's been positioned in the lowest third of the oven, then turn the temperature up to 500 degrees Fahrenheit. Allow the stone to heat up to a temperature of 500 degrees for 20 minutes.

Do you like to cook your pizza on the grill instead? On a surface that has been lightly greased, roll out the pizza dough into a circle of 12 to 14 inches in diameter (depending on the size of your stone). Move onto a pizza peel that has been gently dusted with flour (or inverted baking sheet). The remaining 1 tablespoon of oil should be brushed onto the dough. The pizza should be slid onto the heated stone. Bake for 8 to 10 minutes, or until the topping is brown and crispy. While that happens, add the red cabbage and napa cabbage, carrot, mint, scallions, and pepper to the chicken, and toss to incorporate. After the crust has finished baking, move it to a large cutting board and set it aside to cool for 5 minutes. Make a mound of the salad in the center, then top it with the mango, and serve it right away.

Vietnamese Rice Noodle Salad

Preparation time: 15 minutes
Nutrition facts (per serving): 432 Cal (5.3g fat, 6.6g protein, 2g fiber)

A crisp and energizing salad that's packed to the brim with delicious ingredients!" On a warm day, this is a refreshing salad to have.

Ingredients (4 servings)
Dressing
⅔ cup of fish sauce
½ cup of warm water
6 tablespoons of lime juice
5 tablespoons of sugar
3 fresh chili peppers (Thai, serrano, jalapeño), seeded and minced
2 cloves of garlic, minced

Salad
3 carrots, large, peeled and grated
1 cucumber, large, peeled, seeded, and cut into matchsticks
¼ cup of peanuts, roasted and unsalted
1 chili pepper (Thai, serrano, or jalapeno), seeded and chopped
8 oz. of dried vermicelli noodles
4 cups of leaf lettuce, red or green, chopped
½ cup of basil, chopped
½ cup of cilantro, chopped
½ cup of mint, chopped

Preparation

To make the dressing, whisk together all of the ingredients until the sugar is completely dissolved, then put the dressing aside. To prepare the salad, mix together the carrots, cucumbers, peanuts, and chiles in a quarter cup of the dressing, and then put this mixture aside. After bringing 4 quarts of water to a boil, removing the pot from the heat, adding the noodles, and let the mixture to stand while being stirred regularly for 10 minutes.

After draining the noodles, place them in a significant serving dish. On top of it, layer the carrot combination that has been marinated, followed by lettuce, basil, cilantro, and mint. After pouring half of the remaining dressing over the noodle salad, tossing it to blend the flavors, and dividing it among four salad plates, the salad is ready to serve. Peanuts should be sprinkled on top, and the leftover dressing should be served on the side.

Vietnamese Salad Rolls

Preparation time: 20 minutes
Cook time: 5 minutes
Nutrition facts (per serving): 187 Cal (1.5g fat, 11.6g protein, 3g fiber)

A great and mild starter to start with. The filling for these delectable rice wraps includes noodles, shrimp, carrots, lettuce, and basil. It is possible to use cooked chicken or beef in place of the shrimp. These Vietnamese Salad Rolls are very simple to make and include wonderful, fresh ingredients throughout. Here's the ideal dish for an appetizer to enjoy throughout the spring and summer months.

Ingredients (8 servings)
Large Shrimp
1 (8 oz.) package rice vermicelli
8 oz. cooked, peeled shrimp, cut in half lengthwise
8 rice wrappers
1 carrot, julienned
1 cup shredded lettuce
¼ cup chopped fresh basil
½ cup hoisin sauce
Water, as needed

Preparation
Bring water to a boil in a big stockpot that's been halfway filled with it. After adding the shrimp to the water, simmer them for approximately five minutes, tossing them regularly, until opaque and completely cooked through. After being rinsed, lay the shrimp in a basin and cover it with

ice water. After 10 minutes, drain the shrimp and set them aside. Put the shredded lettuce, chopped cilantro, mint, and scallions into a bowl of a suitable size, and then mix them all together to incorporate them before setting them aside. Prepare your work area before continuing. Distribute the shrimp, lettuce mix, rice noodles, bean sprouts, and rice paper wrappers across the various areas of your station. Put ⅔3 of the way up a very large dish with hot water from the faucet. This basin should be big enough to immerse the wrappers. Put one rice paper wrapper into the water and let it sit there for 30 seconds to 1 minute, or until it becomes pliable and soft.

Put the wrapper down on the clean surface of your workplace. A portion of the lettuce mixture should be placed on the bottom ⅓ of the wrapper. Next, the noodles and the sprouts should be added. Fold the bottom of the wrapper over the filling and secure it with a few folds. After positioning the shrimp so they're centered in the wrapper. Then immediately next to the fold, fold in the side flaps. Keep rolling the wrapper firmly until it can no longer be opened and is completely secure. While you roll the other items, set this one aside on a sheet tray. Mix the hoisin sauce, peanut butter, rice wine vinegar, soy sauce, sesame oil, garlic powder, and onion powder together in a dish of medium size using a whisk. This will form the dipping sauce. The dipping sauce should be served on the side beside the spring rolls.

Beef Salad

Preparation time: 10 minutes

Cook time: 10 minutes

Nutrition facts (per serving): 319 Cal (11g fat, 20g protein, 4g fiber)

Ingredients (4 servings)

2 rump steaks

2 medium carrots, peeled and cut into julienne strips

1 large cucumber, sliced into ribbons with a veg peeler

2 baby gem lettuce, roughly chopped

Handful of fresh coriander, roughly chopped

10-15 fresh mint, leaves torn

Red chili, finely sliced with seeds left in

1 cup dried rice noodles

Beef Marinade

Juice of 2 limes

1 teaspoon fish sauce

1 teaspoon garlic ginger paste

Dressing

2 tablespoon sesame oil

Juice of 1 lime

1 teaspoon fish sauce

1 tablespoon honey

Preparation

Combine the juice from 2 limes, 1 teaspoon of fish sauce, and 1 teaspoon of garlic ginger paste in a mixing bowl. After bringing the steaks to room temperature, pour the marinade over them, cover, and let them soak for at least 20 minutes. Put the noodles in a bowl and cover them with water that's already boiling. After letting it soak for a minute, drain it and give it a quick rinse under cold running water.

After peeling, slicing, and chopping the lettuce, herbs, and chili pepper, add the prepared ingredients in a big dish with the cooled noodles. Wrap it up, then put it in the refrigerator. Using a heated griddle pan, sear the meat for 3 to 4 minutes on each side (for pink in the middle). Cooking times and recommendations for steak. Wrap the cooked steaks in foil in a loose manner and allow them to rest for 3 to 5 minutes.

Combine 1 tablespoon of honey, 1 teaspoon of fish sauce, the juice of 1 lime, and 2 tablespoons of sesame oil in a mixing bowl. Combine thoroughly. Toss the noodles and the chopped salad together, and then divide the mixture among the four bowls. The steak should be sliced very thinly before being placed on top of the salad in each bowl. After pouring it over the salad, the Asian salad dressing should be served.

Desserts

Vietnamese Sweet Corn Pudding

Preparation time: 10 minutes

Cook time: 20 minutes

Nutrition facts (per serving): 252 Cal (18.4g fat, 3.3g protein, 1.1g fiber)

Corn contributes sweetness, juiciness, and crispness to this delicious Vietnamese dessert soup, which is called Sweet Corn Pudding. It's traditionally eaten warm or cold with a sauce made of creamy coconut, and it's offered with the dish. This sweet treat doesn't include any animal products, gluten, or dairy products by design.

Ingredients (10 servings)

3 large ears corn, shucked

4 cups water

2 pandan leaves, tied together and knotted (optional)

¼ cup small tapioca pearls

2 (14-oz.) cans coconut milk

½ cup granulated sugar

Pinch salt

2 tablespoons toasted sesame seeds

Preparation

To remove the kernels from each ear of corn, place it upright in a bowl and, while holding it firmly, use a sharp chef's knife to run down the length of the ear, shaving them off. Set the kernels aside. Put the corn cobs, the pandan leaves (if using), and the water in a pot and bring it to a boil. Cover, bring the heat down, and let it simmer for half an hour. In the meanwhile, add cold water to a small dish large enough to cover the tapioca pearls by half an inch and let them rest.

Take out the corn cobs and pandan leaves and discard them from the saucepan. In the saucepan, mix sugar, maize kernels, coconut milk, and a bit of salt by stirring all of the ingredients together. Bring back up to a boil, then reduce heat to low and simmer for approximately 10 minutes, or until the corn is soft. Have a taste, and if necessary, adjust the amount of sugar and salt.

Tapioca pearls should be added to the saucepan, and the heat should be reduced to a simmer for 2 minutes. Take the food away from the heat to chill it. Can be stored in the refrigerator for up to 2 days. If it becomes too sticky and thick, water may be used to dilute it. You may serve this dish either hot or cold in bowls or glasses. Just before serving, sprinkle some toasted sesame seeds on top.

Vietnamese Vanilla Sponge Cake (Bánh Bông Lan)

Preparation time: 15 minutes
Cook time: 25 minutes
Nutrition facts (per serving): 200 Cal (10g fat, 5 g protein, 1 g fiber)

Banh Bong Lan is a Vietnamese sponge cake with French influences. Eggs, flour, sugar, and vanilla are the main ingredients. In Vietnamese, "orchid cake" is known as Banh Bong Lan. The cake looks like a flowering orchid because of the beaten egg whites. Baking powder may sometimes be used to increase the stability and lift of the mixture.

Ingredients (8 servings)

5 large eggs (separate yolks and whites and bring to room temperature)
½ cup granulated white sugar
1 teaspoon vanilla paste
¼ cup whole milk
¼ cup oil
1 cup all-purpose flour
1-½ teaspoons baking powder
¼ teaspoon salt
¼ teaspoon cream of tartar
Powdered sugar, optional

Preparation

The oven should be preheated at 350 degrees Fahrenheit, In a medium-sized dish, combine the egg yolks, sugar, and vanilla extract and whisk until smooth. Take a bowl, add the oil and milk, and whisk until the mixture is smooth and creamy. Sift flour, baking powder, and salt into a large bowl. Add the flour mixture to the egg mixture and stir well. Make sure all of the batter has been mixed evenly by continuing to mix.

Begin with making the meringue: Egg whites and cream of tartar may be whipped by hand or with the help of a stand mixer with a whisk attachment. Egg whites will become foamy when whisked at high speed after being whisked at moderate speed at first. To get firm peaks, keep on whisking. Add a third of the meringue to the batter at a time. Fold in the meringue with a gentle, steady motion. The meringue can deflate if it's overmixed, so be careful. Spray a 10-inch cake pan with a non-stick baking spray and line the bottom and sides with parchment paper, then bake as instructed.

Mix in the batter and smooth out the surface. To get rid of any air bubbles, gently drop the pan. Make a water bath by putting the pan in a bigger pan. Bake for 25-30 minutes in a water bath pan filled with 1 inch of water. Insert a long skewer into the cake's middle to check for doneness. The cake is done when the toothpick inserted into the center comes out clean. Slowly remove the cake from the oven once it has finished baking. If not, the cake will swiftly lose its volume. To remove the cake from the pan, gently tilt the pan from side to side when it has cooled. Remove the parchment paper from the sides and bottom of the cake. Pour powdered sugar on top of the cake before serving (optional).

Vietnamese Fruit Cocktail (Chè Thái Recipe)

Preparation time: 20 minutes
Cook time: 10 minutes
Nutrition facts (per serving): 319 Cal (11g fat, g protein, 4g fiber)

Sweet lychee bits, jackfruit slices, chewy jellies, and chilly coconut milk all on one spoon... doesn't its sound refreshing? When it comes to Chè Thái, you're not just getting a sweet soup or fruit cocktail; you're getting a dessert that's packed with taste.

Ingredients (10 servings)

1 (20 oz.) can whole water chestnut you only need half
Red food coloring
1 cup tapioca starch
Water, as needed
Ice, as needed

Che Thai

1 (20 oz.) can jackfruit
1 (20 oz.) can lychee
1 (20 oz.) can longan
1 (19 oz.) can ai-yu jelly
1 (20 oz.) can toddy palm seeds
1 coconut, only juice and meat
1 (13.5 oz.) can coconut milk

Preparation

Drain the water from the water chestnut can. Approximately half of the water chestnuts will be sufficient for this recipe. Place the water chestnuts in a large dish and dice them into 14-inch chunks (the coating of the tapioca starch will make them bigger).

To the little bits, add a few drops of red food coloring and completely combine. Tapioca starch will become especially gummy if there's excess water or food coloring in the dish. Make sure the water chestnuts are completely covered with tapioca starch. Place the water chestnuts in a colander and sift to remove any excess starch. Extra starch in the boiling water will also make it gooey, so be sure to keep it out.

Over medium-high heat, bring a saucepan of water to a boil with approximately 2 inches of water in it. The water chestnuts should be added to the mixture in small batches and stirred constantly to prevent them from sticking. Remove the chestnuts from the boiling water and place them in an ice water bath to prevent them from sticking together. Make sure they're in the tub for at least 10 minutes.

Assemble

Save the syrup from one can in a separate container after opening all the canned fruit. I reserve this syrup since I like lychee the most. We discovered that if you combine the syrup from all the cans, the flavor can get mixed. Slice the jackfruit, lychee, and toddy palm into various sizes and thicknesses.

Because longans are little, it's important to keep them as they were when they were first picked. In a big container, combine all of the fruit. Slice the flesh off the coconut and put aside the liquid. Combine the coconut milk and the coconut juice in a separate container. You should begin by adding 12 a cup of juice syrup at a time to the milk to sweeten it.

Adjust according to your preference. Into a big container of fruit add the coconut milk, juice, and meat. I like to chill the chè Thái for a few hours before serving, but crushed ice may be added if you want to serve it right away.

Three Color Dessert (Che Ba Mau)

Preparation time: 30 minutes
Cook time: 45 minutes
Nutrition facts (per serving): 524 Cal (10g fat, 10g protein, 10g fiber)

Easy Three-Color Treat (Che Ba Mau) recipe encapsulates the summery aromas in a cold dessert. This colorful, tiered dish, which goes by the name "Rainbow Dessert," is light, sweet, and packed with a variety of interesting textures. On a hot summer day, there's nothing better than savoring this icy, sweet delight.

Ingredients (4 servings)
3 ½ cups water
1 ½ tablespoon agar powder
½ cup sugar
¼ teaspoon pandan paste

Red Layer
15.5 oz can red beans
1 ½ cups water
¾ cup sugar

Yellow Layer
1 cup mashed mung bean
3 tablespoons sugar

Topping

½ cup coconut sauce

4 cups crushed ice

Preparation

Add the agar powder to the water in a medium saucepan. Using a blender, combine the powder and water and mix well. (Until the powder is heated, it won't dissolve entirely.) Allow the mixture to sit for 15 minutes. Stirring frequently, bring the mixture to a simmer over medium heat. Add the sugar as soon as it begins to boil, then turn off the heat. The sugar should be completely dissolved in around 2-3 minutes of stirring. Using a sieve or spoon, remove the froth and discard it. Add the pandan paste and thoroughly mix it in the mixture before serving. In a medium dish or basin, pour the jelly mixture. Skim the jelly's surface of bubbles using a spoon. Let cool for an hour on the counter. Refrigerate for at least 4 hours to set up.

Run a knife along the edge of the set pandan jelly. Cut the jelly into bars that are about 1 ½ to 2 inches thick, and serve. Use a mandolin to grate the jelly. The thickest shreds may be achieved by using a blade with the fewest teeth. Wait until you're ready to serve before putting it in the fridge.

Red Layer

Remove the canning liquid by rinsing the red beans several times in cool water. In a medium bowl, rinse and drain the paste. Add the water to a small pot and bring it to a boil. Stir in the sugar for a few minutes until it's completely dissolved. Combine the red beans and syrup in a large bowl. Serve the dessert after the red beans have had time to soak in the syrup.

Yellow Layer

Add the sugar and mashed mung beans to a small bowl and mix well. Blend until well-combined and creamy. Serve immediately after removing from the heat. It's time to dish out the three-color dessert! Add ½ cup broken ice to a transparent glass or dessert plate to serve the dessert. A further half-cup of crushed ice and 2-3 tablespoons of pandan jelly will round out the flavor profile. A generous dollop of coconut sauce on top completes the dish. Enjoy your meal as soon as possible. If you have any leftovers, keep them in the fridge and eat them within the week.

Vietnamese Honeycomb Cake (Banh Bo Nuong)

Preparation time: 20 minutes
Cook time: 40 minutes
Nutrition facts (per serving): 303 Cal (5g fat, 40g protein, 2g fiber)

Banh Bo Nuong, a Vietnamese honeycomb cake, is one of the country's most popular desserts. If you cut a cross section of the cake, you'll find a honeycomb-like structure generated by pockets of expanding gas.

Ingredients (8 servings)

½ teaspoon canola oil

1 cup coconut cream

¼ teaspoon salt

½ teaspoon pandan extract or vanilla extract

5 ½ oz. white caster sugar or brown sugar

1 tablespoon canola oil

5 large eggs, at room temperature

6 oz. tapioca starch (available at Asian groceries)

2 teaspoon rice flour (available at Asian groceries)

2 teaspoon cream of tartar

1 teaspoon bicarb soda

Preparation

Set the oven to fan-forced 356 F. When the oven is preheated to 380°F, grease the bottom of an 8 inch round cake pans with the ½ teaspoon of oil. Add the coconut cream and salt to a mixing dish. Add white caster sugar and pandan essence if creating the pandan variant. If you're preparing the brown sugar version, you'll also want to stir in some vanilla extract and brown sugar. Take out of the microwave and stir for a minute. Set aside the tablespoon of canola oil.

Crack the eggs in a separate basin. Cut the yolks into little pieces using scissors. Incorporate the eggs into the coconut mixture. Mix the egg mixture with half of the tapioca starch and rice flour and gently whisk until the mixture is smooth. Whisk for a further minute after adding the remaining tapioca starch and flour. Add the cream of tartar and bicarbonate of soda by sifting them both in. 30 seconds is about right for a mix.

The cake pan should be placed on a heat-resistant surface once it has been removed from the oven. Pour the cake batter onto a heated cake pan after pressing it through a sieve. The cake tin should be dropped many times onto the counter from a height of about 1 inch in order to remove the air bubbles. Bake the cake for 40 minutes in the oven. In order to set up a cooling station, you'll need a cooling rack and something to raise it off the ground.

See the image above to get an idea of what I'm talking about. This is to prevent condensation from forming on the cake while it cools upside down. The cake should be removed from the oven and placed upside-down on a cooling rack immediately after 40 minutes. Remove the cake from the pan after approximately 45 minutes of cooling or when the cake is lukewarm.

Sesame Balls Recipe
(Vietnamese Bánh Cam)

Preparation time: 3 hours
Cook time: 40 minutes
Nutrition facts (per serving): 186 Cal (1g fat, 5g protein, 3g fiber)

This recipe for sesame balls, also known as Vietnamese bánh cam, satisfies the need for a snack by combining a golden crispy outer shell made of glutinous rice with a filling made of sweet mung beans and a coating of white sesame seeds.

Ingredients (8 servings)
4 oz dried mung beans
¾ oz. sugar
¼ teaspoon salt, optional
A dash of vanilla extract, optional

Outer Shell (Vỏ)
½ cup warm water plus more on the side for later
1 ½ oz. sugar
½ teaspoon salt
4 oz. glutinous rice flour
¾ oz. rice flour
¾ oz. all-purpose wheat flour
5 tablespoons potato flakes
1 ½ teaspoon baking powder

Preparation

Like rice, mung beans should be rinsed and drained under running water. Prepare the mung beans by soaking them overnight in water. To prepare, bring a pot of salted water to a boil, then pour over the mung beans, cover, and refrigerate overnight. Once the liquid has cooled, you may drain it to speed things up (about 2 hours, then repeat this process 2 more times).

Take out the mung beans and cook them. On medium heat, a steamer is the best technique to ensure that your food is cooked to perfection. With little more water than you would need to create a cup of rice, you can prepare it in a rice cooker, but it will lose some of its adhering to the pot. It's time to mash the beans when they're no longer crunchy and have softened. With a stovetop steamer, this took me around 25 minutes. Add the sugar, salt, and vanilla to the cooked mung beans and mix well. Make a thick and somewhat dry mixture by mashing and adding water, as necessary.

Outer Shell (Vô)

Pour half of the water into a large container. Mix in the sugar and salt until they are completely dissolved. Add the rest of the ingredients and stir well (you can use a food processor if you want). Ideally, the dough should be somewhat dry and resemble play dough. Rest the dough for at least 2 hours, but preferably 8. After resting, it'll rise slightly and hydrate, making it simpler to handle.

Bnh Cam

Put the mung bean filling in a disk of dough and flatten it out. There is no right or wrong answer when it comes to the dough to filling ratio. I like a diameter of around 1 inch, although you may go larger if you choose. During the cooking process, they'll slightly expand. Since the dough will already be expanding and adding air to the middle, make sure there are no air pockets within. Close the ball up so that it doesn't split. Sesame seeds may be used to coat the balls after they have been softly rolled in your palms. Prepare to fry.

Frying

Deep fry the bánh Cam in a saucepan of neutral cooking oil heated to 285 degrees Fahrenheit. Make sure there isn't too much food in the pot. For each batch, it should take roughly 11 minutes. For even cooking, you may have to move them around a lot.

Pandan Coconut Jelly

Preparation time: 30 minutes

Cook time: 20 minutes

Nutrition facts (per serving): 235 Cal (10g fat, 1g protein, 1g fiber)

Wun Gati Bai Tuey (Coconut and Pandan Jelly) is as much fun to create as it is to savor! Featuring two distinct flavors, it's a beautiful and delicious treat that everyone will enjoy. Coconut milk, pandan flavoring, and agar-agar make up Pandan Coconut Jelly, an incredibly flavorful treat. It's as much fun to prepare as it is to eat, thanks to the two brightly colored layers!

Ingredients (12 servings)

1 package clear agar-agar bars

3 cups water

1 cup sugar

1 can (19 oz.) coconut milk

Pandan Layer

1 package green agar-agar bars

3 cups water

2 cups coconut juice

1 cup sugar

1 tablespoon pandan extract

Preparation

Thinly slice the clear glycerol agar-agar bars for serving. Add the agar-agar and water to a saucepan and bring to a boil. Soak for 30 minutes at the very least. Thinly slice green agar-agar bars. Combine the water and coconut juice in a separate saucepan and bring to a boil. Allow 30 minutes of soaking time. To make the clear agar-agar mixture, bring it to a boil over medium heat, stirring often, until all of the agar-agar is dissolved.

Stir in the sugar until it is completely dissolved. Cook for another 10 to 12 minutes. Reduce the heat and add the coconut milk. Cook for 2 to 3 minutes on low heat. Then, in a 9 x 13 inch pan, spread the mixture evenly. Pop any bubbles with a toothpick. Allow the coconut layer to harden before moving on to the next layer. Bring the green agar-agar mixture to a boil over medium heat, stirring constantly, until the agar-agar melts.

Stir in the sugar until completely dissolved. Stir in the pandan extract and mix well. Continue to cook for another 10 to 15 minutes, if possible. Wait until you're ready to pour it atop the coconut layer to keep it heated on the burner. Gently pour the pandan layer on top of the coconut layer when it's firm to the touch but still slightly warm. Pop any bubbles with a toothpick. Refrigerate the jelly to firm it up fully. To serve, loosen the jelly with the edge of a blunt knife. Cut into serving sizes by carefully inverting onto a serving plate.

Bánh Tiêu (Vietnamese Donuts)

Preparation time: 15 minutes
Cook time: 10 minutes
Nutrition facts (per serving): 212 Cal (11g fat, 15g protein, 3g fiber)

Hollow-inside sesame brioches that are soft and fluffy are just waiting for your favorite filling! A savory sauce or even a chocolate spread are all possibilities! On their own, these fried brioches are a delectable treat.

Ingredients (6 servings)

1 ⅓ cup all-purpose flour

¾ teaspoon baking powder

¼ teaspoon salt

½ cup and 2 tablespoons almond milk at room temperature (or other plant-based milk)

2 ½ tablespoons sugar

1 teaspoon dry yeast

½ teaspoon vanilla extract

¼ cup white sesame seeds

1 ½ cup of oil, for frying

Preparation

Whisk together the flour, baking powder, and salt in a large basin. 2 tablespoons of almond milk, sugar, dry yeast, and vanilla essence should be combined in a small dish. Add the remaining almond milk and vanilla essence to the flour mixture and stir until well-combined. The dough should be smooth and slightly sticky after kneading for 5-7 minutes. If it's too wet, add a tablespoon of flour at a time until it's the right consistency. Add extra almond milk if it's too thick.

To protect the dough, wrap it in plastic wrap and leave it in a warm area until it has doubled in size, approximately 1 hour and 30 minutes. Make 6 equal-sized balls out of the deflated dough. To flatten the balls, roll them in white sesame seeds and then pat them out to a thickness of 3-4 millimeters. Repeat the process with the remaining balls. Add the oil to a large saucepan and bring it to a boil over medium heat. Focus on 1 disc at a time, using 2 wooden spatulas (or chopsticks) to rotate it every 5-7 seconds while the oil is heated.

The disc will begin to become a golden brown and blow out like a balloon as it oxidizes. Remove from the oil when it's golden brown and transfer to a dish lined with kitchen paper towel to remove any excess oil. Make a second set by repeating Step 2. You may eat it as is, or cut it open and stuff it with chocolate spread or caramel sauce! These donuts are best served fresh, but they may be stored at room temperature in an airtight container for up to 2 days.

Vietnamese Jello Mooncakes

Preparation time: 5 minutes
Cook time: 1 hour
Nutrition facts (per serving): 139 Cal (10g fat, 10g protein, 2g fiber)

The traditional Mid-Autumn Festival mooncakes have been replaced with Jell-O mooncakes in my home. The outside layer of these Jell-O mooncakes is coconut cream, while the interior filling is taro and green tea.

Ingredients (12 servings)
1 pack of agar-agar powder
1 (14 oz.) can of coconut cream
2 cups sugar
7 cups cold water
2 tablespoons purple taro powder or matcha milk tea powder
12 molds, for outer layer
12 molds, for filling
1 baking tray, enough to fit the 12 filling molds

Preparation
On a tabletop, spread out all of the molds. Make sure the molds are in the baking pan. Preparation of the condiments. In a dish, combine purple taro powder and water. Add the water, coconut cream, sugar, and agar-agar powder to a saucepan and bring to a boil. Mix thoroughly. About 20 minutes after mixing, let the agar-agar mixture cool completely before using it.

Powdering The Agar-Agar

After 20 minutes, bring the agar-agar mixture to a boil on the burner. High-heat cooking may begin. To keep the agar-agar mixture from adhering to the bottom of the pot, you must constantly swirl it while it is on the burner. Continue cooking for another 2 minutes, then turn off the heat once the agar-agar mixture reaches a boil. It's best to maintain the heat at the "keep warm" setting if your stove has one. As an alternative, you may add hot water to a bigger pot, and then put the pot with agar-agar mixture inside of it to keep it warm.

Filling

Then, to the bowl of purple taro powder, add the agar-agar mixture, which should now contain 2 cups. To prevent the mixture from solidifying, whisk it constantly. Filling molds with a flurry after quickly pouring the contents into them. Adding cold water to the tray beneath the molds can speed up the hardening process of the Jell-O.

Outer Layer

Make sure the agar-agar mixture hasn't started to solidify before proceeding. Make sure it's boiling again before turning the heat back down to "keep warm," if necessary. Confirm to quickly fill the molds with the agar-agar mixture. Each mold should be filled with an agar-agar mixture as it starts to firm. To finish things off, add the remainder of the agar-agar mixture to the mold. Refrigerate when the Jell-O has hardened and cooled down.

Vietnamese Glutinous Rice Balls (Chè Trôi Nước)

Preparation time: 30 minutes
Cook time: 1 hour
Nutrition facts (per serving): 489 Cal (6g fat, 11g protein, 5g fiber)

Only in Grandma's kitchen will you discover a recipe for Vietnamese Glutinous Rice Balls like this! The creamiest mung bean filling has been simmered for hours until it's just right. A creamy coconut cream is then drizzled on top for the ultimate velvety dessert experience!

Ingredients (servings)
Rice Balls
1.1 lb. glutinous rice flour
2 cups water

Mung Bean Paste
⅔ lb. mung beans
3 cup water
1 ½ teaspoon salt, or to taste
½ tablespoon sugar, or to taste
½ cup oil

Ginger Syrup and Coconut Cream
1 lb. palm sugar
1 pandan leaf
5 teaspoons ginger

3 ½ cups cup water

1 cup coconut cream

½ teaspoon salt, or to taste

White sesame seeds (for sprinkling on top)

Preparation

The first step is to make the dough. Refrigerate after thoroughly mixing the flour and water. You will need to let it rise overnight or for at least 30 minutes. Add the water to the mung beans and bring to a boil. It should be brought to a boil, then simmered for at least 30 minutes, or until the liquid has evaporated completely.

Stir in the salt and the mung beans until well combined. Serve at room temperature. To make the filling silky-smooth, pulse the mung beans in a food processor until smooth. Add the mung bean processed to the oil in a skillet and heat through. Add the sugar and stir until it forms a dough. Spring onion heads, thinly cut, are an optional extra for some families. Refrigerate the mung bean paste balls once they've cooled to stiffen them up.

It's time to cook today! Remove the dough from the refrigerator and re-knead it. Knead in 1 tablespoon water every batch until you get the desired consistency. Boiled water in a huge pot. Place a big dish of ice water next to the pot to keep it cool. Form a ball out of the dough. Press your hands together and flatten out. A mung bean ball should be placed in the middle. Using your hands, roll the dough around the filling until it's fully encasing it. Roll it one more time to remove any wrinkles.

As you're forming the balls, carefully set them in the pot of hot water. As soon as they begin to float, they'll be ready. Pour the cooled water over each cooked ball. To keep the balls from clinging to one other, keep adding cold water to the container. Touching them should be a pleasant experience. Bring the water, palm sugar, and ginger to a boil in a small saucepan to prepare the ginger syrup, then remove from the heat. Simmer for 15 minutes and then serve.

Put the coconut milk and salt in a pot and tie the pandan leaf into a knot. Add water and bring it to a boil. Toast the sesame seeds to a golden-brown color before adding them to the dish.

Pour the ginger syrup into the dish that has been drained of its water and the rice balls will be ready in no time. Toasted sesame seeds and pandan-infused coconut cream should be sprinkled on top of the dish before it is served.

Taro and Sweet Potato Balls Dessert

Preparation time: 1 hour 30 minutes
Cook time: 15 minutes
Nutrition facts (per serving): 548 Cal (1g fat, 8g protein, 10g fiber)

Every sugar need will be satisfied by this original Taiwanese dessert! These delicious taro and sweet potato balls are created with just whole, unprocessed foods. The only other thing that will elevate your dessert soup to a whole new level is to eat it with a calming ginger syrup!

Ingredients (6 servings)
½ lb. taro, peeled and sliced
½ lb. orange sweet potato, peeled and sliced
½ lb. purple sweet potato, peeled and sliced
1 lb. tapioca starch
5 tablespoons sugar, or to taste
Water, if needed

Red Bean
1 lb. adzuki red bean (pre-soaked)
2 oz. rock sugar, or to taste
8 cups water

Ginger Syrup
5 slices ginger
2 oz. rock sugar, or to taste
4 cups water

Preparation

Steam the sweet potatoes and taro slices for 30 minutes each in a steamer that has been set up. With a bigger steamer, you can steam more food at once. Steamed sweet potatoes are followed by steamed taro pieces, which are mashed together with a fork. A dough is made when 3 ½ oz. tapioca starch and 1 teaspoon sugar are added to taro pulp. To be able to hold its shape as a ball, it should be firm but not so sticky that it adheres to your fingers.

You may require a different quantity of tapioca starch depending on what kind of sweet potato or taro you use. Add a tablespoon of water at a time until you reach the right consistency if the dough is too dry. Additionally, using less starch will provide an easier-to-bite ball, while using more starch will result in a chewier ball and a milder flavor, respectively. As with the mashed purple and orange sweet potatoes, use extra tapioca starch to thicken the mixture since they're naturally more water-rich.

Roll ⅔ inch logs of dough using tiny handfuls of dough ") as the diameter. Slice the wood into ⅔ inch pieces using a knife. To prevent the balls from sticking together, sprinkle them with tapioca starch. Prepare a big bowl of room temperature water and a saucepan of boiling water. A handful of uncooked pieces may be added to a pot of boiling water to simmer until they float. Transfer them to the water bowl after another 2 minutes of cooking. The remaining sugar, 1 tablespoon each batch, should be added to the scooped-out balls (or to taste).

Red Bean

Red beans should be soaked in water for 3hours. Cooking time will be greatly reduced as a result of this. A saucepan of water and rock sugar is all that's needed for the beans to boil for 30 minutes, or until tender. To serve as a garnish, remove the beans with a spoon. Red bean water may be saved for your dessert soup, if desired.

Soup with Fresh Ginger Simmering in Water

For 30 minutes, bring the water, sugar, and ginger to a boil. Serve.

Cassava and Coconut Milk (Khoai Mi Nuoc Cot Dua)

Preparation time: 5 minutes
Cook time: 8 minutes
Nutrition facts (per serving): 408 Cal (19g fat, 6g protein, 5 g fiber)

If you're in the mood for something sweet, this Cassava and Coconut Milk dish in the Instant Pot is an excellent choice. This meal is bursting with mouthwatering flavors and textures, thanks to the addition of shredded coconut and a sweet and salty nut mix to the creamy cassava chunks. The mix of starchy and crunchy textures in the cassava is just fantastic. It's my go-to snack when I'm in the need for something sweet yet comforting.

Ingredients (servings)
1 lb. frozen peeled cassava, thawed
½ cup coconut milk
1 tablespoon sugar
Pinch of salt

Coconut Topping
1 cup shredded young coconut or ½ cup dried coconut flakes

Sesame Peanut Topping
¼ cup roasted peanuts
2 tablespoons sugar
1 tablespoon roasted sesame seeds
¼ teaspoon salt

Preparation

Sesame Peanut Topping

Add the roasted peanuts to a food processor and pulse until finely ground. Pulse the peanuts 3 to 4 times to pulverize them. Salt, sugar, and toasted sesame seeds are all that are needed. To complete the mixing, pulse the ingredients a final 4-5 times. Set aside in a small dish for the time being.

Cassava Sauce

In a medium dish, combine the thawed cassava and water. Pat dry with a towel after rinsing with cold water. It is best to split the cassava in half lengthwise and then cut into smaller pieces. Take out the pieces and put them in a steam basket.

In a 6-quart Instant Pot, add 1 cup of water to the inner pot. Take out the steamer basket and place the cassava in the inside pot. Close the lid and turn the handle to "Sealing" to keep the contents safe. For an 8-minute cook time, set the pressure cooker on high.

Cooking time is complete, and the pressure should be manually released. The inner pot's steamer basket should be removed and placed on the counter for use. To remove the fibrous spine from the middle of each cassava piece, delicately pull it out with your fingers.

Saucing The Coconut

Empty the inner pot of water. Press the "Sauté" button on your keyboard. Add the sugar and the salt to the inner pot. Mix the items together using a spoon. Add the cooked cassava to the boiling coconut milk. Coat the cassava in the coconut milk, stirring gently after each addition. A few minutes of simmering will help the coconut milk to thicken. To exit the Sauté mode, use the "Cancel" button.

Place on a big dish and serve. Sprinkle the cassava with coconut flakes or shredded fresh coconut. Spread the sesame peanut topping generously on top of the salad. Take advantage of the weather while you can. Keep any leftovers in the refrigerator and eat them within 3-4 days.

Steamed Vegan Rice Cakes
Banh Bo Hap

Preparation time: 10 minutes

Cook time: 15 minutes

Nutrition facts (per serving): 334 Cal (8.5g fat, 4g protein, g fiber)

A simple recipe for banh bo hap, also known as steamed rice cake, is a vegan treat that's fluffy, sweet, and quite stunning in appearance. The kids will have a good time making it, and it won't cost you much money.

Ingredients (12 servings)

4 cups rice flour

2 cups lukewarm water

1 (14 oz.) can coconut milk

1 cup white sugar

4 teaspoons tapioca starch

1 ½ teaspoons active dry yeast

½ teaspoon vanilla extract

¼ teaspoon salt

2 teaspoons oil, or as needed

Preparation

In a bowl, thoroughly combine the rice flour, water, coconut milk, sugar, tapioca starch, yeast, vanilla extract, and salt. Whisk until smooth. Use a lid to cover it. Allow the batter to rest for approximately 2 hours, or until air bubbles float to the top. Stir thoroughly. Oil the cavities of the cake molds. Put a steamer insert into a saucepan, then fill the saucepan with water until it reaches a point that is just below the steamer's base. Put the cake molds on top of the stack, then pour the batter into each one, being sure to leave 1 ¾ inches of room at the top for the cakes to rise. Bring the water up to a rolling boil. Cover and steam for about 10 minutes, or until a toothpick placed into a cake comes out clean.

Vietnamese Donuts (Bánh Tiêu)

Preparation time: 15 minutes
Cook time: 10 minutes
Nutrition facts (per serving): 356 Cal (10g fat, 7g protein, 2g fiber)

Hollow-inside sesame brioches that are soft and fluffy are just waiting for your favorite filling! A savory filling or even a chocolate spread are all possibilities! You can eat these fried brioches on their own, too!

Ingredients (6 servings)

1 ⅓ cup all-purpose flour

¾ teaspoon baking powder

¼ teaspoon salt

½ cup and 2 tablespoons almond milk at room temperature (or other plant-based milk)

2 and ½ tablespoon sugar

1 teaspoon dry yeast

½ teaspoon vanilla extract

¼ cup white sesame seeds

1 and ½ cup of oil, for frying

Preparation

Whisk together the flour, baking powder, and salt in a large basin.2 tablespoons of almond milk, sugar, dry yeast, and vanilla essence should be combined in a small dish. Add the remaining almond milk and vanilla essence to the flour mixture and stir until well-combined. The dough should be smooth and slightly sticky after kneading for 5-7 minutes. If it's too wet, add 1 tablespoon of flour at a time until it's the right consistency. Add extra almond milk if it's too thick.

To prove the dough, wrap it in plastic wrap and leave it in a warm area until it has doubled in size, approximately 1 hour and 30 minutes. Make 6 equal-sized balls from the deflated dough. To flatten the balls, roll them in white sesame seeds and then pat them out to a thickness of ⅕ inch. Repeat the process with the remaining balls.

Add the oil to a large saucepan and bring it to a boil over medium heat. One disc at a time, using 2 wooden spatulas (or chopsticks) to rotate it every 5-7 seconds while the oil is heated. The disc will begin to become a golden brown and blow out like a balloon as it oxidizes. Remove from the oil when it's golden brown and transfer to a dish lined with kitchen paper towel to remove any excess oil. Make a second set by repeating the step.

You may eat it as is, or cut it open and stuff it with chocolate spread or caramel sauce! These donuts are best served fresh, but they may be stored at room temperature in an airtight container for up to 2 days.

Drinks

Vietnamese Coffee

Preparation time: 10 minutes
Nutrition facts (per serving): 158 Cal (5.1 fat, 3.4g protein,0.1 g fiber)

This one is so good, it'll appeal to even the most adamant black coffee drinkers. On a hot winter day, serve it hot. At night, serve it hot as a special treat to your visitors. It was in Vietnam that we discovered this method and now we drink most of our coffee this way.

Ingredients (1 servings)
3 tablespoons Vietnamese ground coffee
1-3 tablespoons sweetened condensed milk
6-8 oz. water that's close to boiling point (depending on your desired coffee strength)

Preparation
For this Vietnamese coffee recipe, 6-oz. Phin Vietnamese coffee filters are available in a variety of sizes to suit your brewing preferences. Alternatively, a French press or your preferred drip coffee technique may be used. Pour 3 tablespoons of coffee grounds into the filter and stir to combine. Avoid shaky or compressed brews, which may cause coffee grounds to fall into the pores of the coffee filter. As a consequence, the coffee may either take an eternity to trickle or the grinds may completely block the filter. To use, carefully place the metal filter on the coffee.

Using a mug or heatproof glass, add the quantity of condensed milk that you want. Measure out 6 oz. of water that's just about boiling. If you like a milder cup of joe, go with 8 oz. instead of 10. Pour 2 teaspoons of boiling water into the coffee filter and wait for 5 seconds to "bloom" the coffee before brewing.

After that, gently squeeze the filter to compact the blooming coffee grounds. When you've used up all of your water, this slows down the drip rate and provides for a more delicious cup of coffee. To get the best brewing time, follow these procedures. The coffee will begin to flow into your cup or glass as you carefully pour the remainder of the water through the filter. To complete the drip brewing process, give it around 5 minutes. Stir in the condensed milk after removing the filter.

Vietnamese Iced Coffee

Preparation time: 2 minutes
Cook time: 5 minutes
Nutrition facts (per serving): 128 Cal (2g fat, 3g protein, 1.2g fiber)

The combination of a strong cup of coffee with condensed milk and ice is an outstanding Southeast Asian dessert. Even those who only drink their coffee black will find this to their liking. Serve it chilled on a hot summer day or as a special treat at night to your guests. In Vietnam, we discovered this technique and now drink most of our espresso this way.

Ingredients (1 servings)
2 tablespoons sweetened condensed milk
1 ½ tablespoon coarse ground coffee (use a roast suitable for espresso)
Hot water (almost to a boil)
Ice, to taste

Preparation
Fill an 8-to-10-oz. glass with sweetened condensed milk. Remove the coffee filter's top screen and discard it. After compacting the coffee grounds, place the filter with the screw screen back on. Put the sweetened condensed milk filter in the glass. Sprinkle the grounds with a little amount of hot water, and then let them rest for 30 seconds.

Allow 2 complete rotations of the filter screen screw. Take out the filter and fill it with hot water to the top, then cover and let it rest for about 5 minutes at a rate of around 3-4 drips per second. Coffee's grind is too coarse if quicker. The grind of the coffee is too fine if the coffee is ground too slowly.) Remove the filter from the glass once the water has flowed through it. Combine the sweetened condensed milk and coffee in a bowl. Enjoy with ice.

Dragon Fruit Shake

Preparation time: 10 minutes
Nutrition facts (per serving): 149 Cal (0.8g fat, g1.4 protein,0.8 g fiber)

I had it at a Vietnamese restaurant in Chinatown. It was delicious, tantalizing, and wonderfully reviving!

Ingredients (1 servings)
2 medium dragon fruits
¼ cup blueberry
4 pieces ice cubes
3 tablespoons condensed milk
1 cup milk

Preparation
Once the dragon fruits have been peeled and sliced into cubes, go to the next step of making the dragon fruit shake. In a separate blender jug, combine the chopped dragon fruit with the sweetened condensed milk, blueberries (or any other berry), crushed ice, and fresh milk; mix for 10 seconds or until it's smooth. Crush a few cubes of ice into the shake before pouring it into a glass.

Triple Fruit Drink

Preparation time: 5 minutes
Nutrition facts (per serving): 92 Cal (0.3g fat, 1g protein, 0.7 g fiber)

This one is an excellent beverage to have with breakfast due to the terrific combination of citrus juices, particularly orange, lemon, and apricot nectar.

Ingredients (4 servings)
1 (12 oz.) can apricot nectar, chilled
1 ½ cups orange juice, chilled
2 tablespoons lemon juice

Preparation
Mix up some apricot nectar, some orange juice, and some lemon juice in a pitcher. Serve cold.

Strawberry Shortcake Drink

Preparation time: 5 minutes
Nutrition facts (per serving): 476 Cal (17.5g fat,5.2 g protein, 2.4g fiber)

This is one of my go-to drinks on a night out with the girls. We like making them at any time of the year, but we find that they taste much better when served on a warm summer day.

Ingredients (1 servings)

¼ cup frozen strawberries, thawed
1 ¼ fluid oz. amaretto liqueur
2 (½ cup) scoops vanilla ice cream
1 dash vanilla extract
½ cup crushed ice
¼ fluid oz. vanilla-flavored vodka
1 tablespoon whipped cream
1 fresh strawberry

Preparation

Put the strawberries, the amaretto liqueur, the vanilla ice cream, the vanilla extract, the crushed ice, and the vanilla vodka into a mixer. Blend until smooth. Cover, and mix until there are no lumps. After you have poured the mixture into the glass, top it with whipped cream and a fresh strawberry.

Refreshing Banana Drink

Preparation time: 10 minutes
Nutrition facts (per serving): 158 Cal (2.4g fat,2.1 g protein, 4.4g fiber)

On a hot day, this is the perfect beverage. In addition to that, it replaces the need for a milkshake made with ice cream! This highly tasty and sweet delicacy that uses natural flavoring may be made by combining almond milk, cinnamon, and bananas in the appropriate proportions.

Ingredients (1 servings)

1 ripe banana
¾ cup almond milk
4 ice cubes
1 dash ground cinnamon
1 dash vanilla extract

Preparation

In a blender, combine the banana, almond milk, ice cubes, cinnamon, and vanilla extract. Blend on medium speed until the mixture is frothy and creamy, which should take around 1 minute.

Pumpkin Spice Protein Drink

Preparation time: 10 minutes
Nutrition facts (per serving): 280 Cal (45.6g fat, g protein, 7.5g fiber)

Those who are often on the run will appreciate this speedy and simple protein drink. The protein powder will help you feel fuller for a longer period of time. You may use 2 tablespoons of peanut butter as a date alternative in this recipe.

Ingredients (servings)
1 cup unsweetened almond milk
2 bananas, sliced and frozen
½ cup canned pumpkin
2 dates, pitted
1 scoop vanilla protein powder
½ teaspoon vanilla extract
1 pinch ground nutmeg
1 pinch ground cinnamon
1 pinch ground cloves
1 pinch ground ginger

Preparation
In a blender, puree the following ingredients until completely smooth: almond milk, bananas, pumpkin, dates, protein powder, vanilla essence, nutmeg, cinnamon, cloves, and ginger.

Chocolate Martini

Preparation time: 2 minutes

Nutrition facts (per serving): 328 Cal (0.2g fat, 0.1g protein, 1.2g fiber)

Creme de cacao and chocolate syrup are combined with ice and vodka in a shaker, and then the mixture is strained into a glass. This cocktail is perfect for those who appreciate a sweet taste in their beverages.

Ingredients (4 servings)

4 (1.5 fluid oz.) vodka

5 (1.5 fluid oz.) cocoa cream liqueur

2 teaspoons chocolate syrup

Preparation

Mix vodka, cocoa cream, and chocolate syrup together in a cocktail mixer that's half-filled with ice. Perform a vigorous shake, then pour the mixture into four cocktail glasses.

Dragon Fruit Cocktail

Preparation time: 10 minutes
Nutrition facts (per serving): 225 Cal (8g fat, 3g protein, 2g fiber)

Have you tried this special dragon fruit cocktail before? Well, now you can enjoy this unique and flavorsome combination by trying this recipe at home.

Ingredients (2 servings)

1 cup dragon fruit, peeled and diced

2 limes

1 teaspoon of honey

1 blood orange

3 ozs. vodka

1 oz. orange liquor

Preparation

Blend the dragon fruit with orange pulp, lime juice, honey, vodka, and orange liquor in a blender. Serve.

Hot Mocha Drink Mix

Preparation time: 10 minutes
Nutrition facts (per serving): 8 Cal (0.6g fat, 0.9g protein, 0.2g fiber)

Here's a deliciously creamy hot beverage mix that's suitable for both children and adults and a snap to create! If you want, you may spice it up with nutmeg or cinnamon.

Ingredients (66 servings)

1 cup white sugar

1 cup dry milk powder

1 cup powdered non-dairy creamer

½ cup unsweetened cocoa

¼ cup instant coffee granules

Preparation

Sugar, milk powder, creamer, cocoa, and instant coffee should all be mixed together in a large dish. Combine everything and stir it up until smooth. Keep in an airtight container until ready to use. To serve, bring one cup of water to a boil for each individual serving (or milk, for a creamier taste.) Mix in around 2 to 3 heaping tablespoons' worth of the cocoa mixture.

If you liked Vietnamese recipes, discover to how cook DELICIOUS recipes from **Balkan** countries!

Within these pages, you'll learn 35 authentic recipes from a Balkan cook. These aren't ordinary recipes you'd find on the Internet, but recipes that were closely guarded by our Balkan mothers and passed down from generation to generation.

Main Dishes, Appetizers, and Desserts included!

If you want to learn how to make Croatian green peas stew, and 32 other authentic Balkan recipes, then start with our book!

Order at www.balkanfood.org/cook-books/ for only $2,99!

If you're a **Mediterranean** dieter who wants to know the secrets of the Mediterranean diet, dieting, and cooking, then you're about to discover how to master cooking meals on a Mediterranean diet right now!

In fact, if you want to know how to make Mediterranean food, then this new e-book - "The 30-minute Mediterranean diet" - gives you the answers to many important questions and challenges every Mediterranean dieter faces, including:

- How can I succeed with a Mediterranean diet?
- What kind of recipes can I make?
- What are the key principles to this type of diet?
- What are the suggested weekly menus for this diet?
- Are there any cheat items I can make?

... and more!

If you're serious about cooking meals on a Mediterranean diet and you really want to know how to make Mediterranean food, then you need to grab a copy of "The 30-minute Mediterranean diet" right now.

Prepare **111 recipes with several ingredients in less than 30 minutes**!

Order at www.balkanfood.org/cook-books/ for only $2,99!

What could be better than a home-cooked meal? Maybe only a **Greek** homemade meal.

Do not get discouraged if you have no Greek roots or friends. Now you can make a Greek food feast in your kitchen.

This ultimate Greek cookbook offers you 111 best dishes of this cuisine! From more famous gyros to more exotic *Kota Kapama* this cookbook keeps it easy and affordable.

All the ingredients necessary are wholesome and widely accessible. The author's picks are as flavorful as they are healthy. The dishes described in this cookbook are "what Greek mothers have made for decades."

Full of well-balanced and nutritious meals, this handy cookbook includes many vegan options. Discover a plethora of benefits of Mediterranean cuisine, and you may fall in love with cooking at home.

Inspired by a real food lover, this collection of delicious recipes will taste buds utterly satisfied.

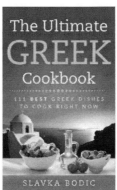

Order at www.balkanfood.org/cook-books/ for only $2,99!

Maybe to try exotic **Syrian** cuisine?

From succulent *sarma*, soups, warm and cold salads to delectable desserts, the plethora of flavors will satisfy the most jaded foodie. Have a taste of a new culture with this **traditional Syrian cookbook**.

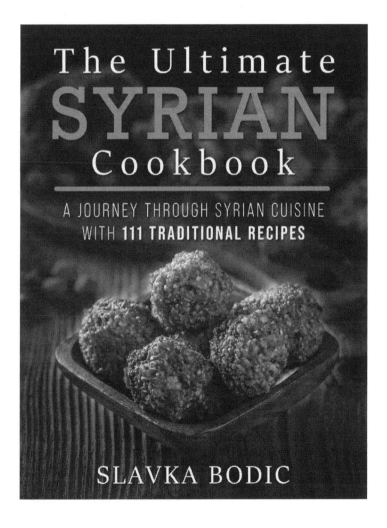

Maybe **Polish** cuisine?

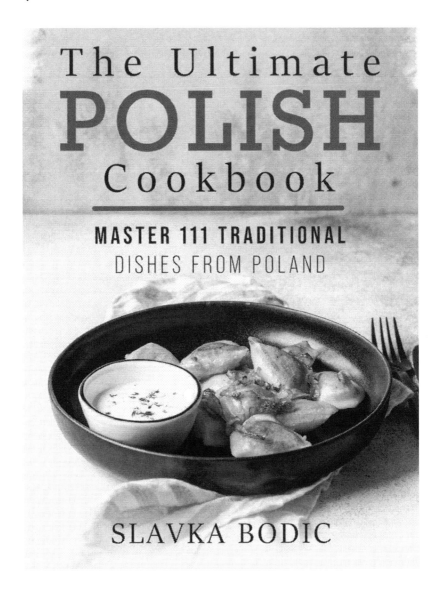

ONE LAST THING

If you enjoyed this book or found it useful, I'd be very grateful if you could find the time to post a short review on Amazon. Your support really does make a difference and I read all the reviews personally, so I can get your feedback and make this book even better.

Thanks again for your support!

Please send me your feedback at

www.balkanfood.org

Made in the USA
Monee, IL
31 May 2023